UNDERSTANDING HISTORY

UNDERSTANDING HISTORY

A PRIMER
OF HISTORICAL METHOD

Louis Gottschalk

UNIVERSITY OF CHICAGO

NEW YORK · ALFRED A. KNOPF
1951

THIS IS A BORZOI BOOK,
PUBLISHED BY ALFRED A. KNOPF, INC.

PUBLISHED OCTOBER 23, 1950
SECOND PRINTING, NOVEMBER 1951

TO *my friends and colleagues*

WILLIAM THOMAS HUTCHINSON
AND
JAMES LEA CATE

who for several years have shared with me the pain and pleasure of giving THE LABORATORY COURSE IN HISTORICAL METHOD, *where I learned much of what has been set forth in this book.*

PREFACE

Since 1933 I have collaborated with various colleagues in the teaching of a "Laboratory Course in Historical Method." The word "laboratory" in the title of that course is taken seriously. Each student is expected to do as much of his work as possible in the presence of the others and of the professor. Since little serious historical research can be done without an adequate library, much of the actual note-taking and writing has to take place before the work is submitted for the criticism of the class, but in class, subjects, methods, tools, and the theoretical problems of the students are discussed as the occasions arise. Neither questions regarding causality, frames of reference, and the philosophy of history nor analyses of the major controversies of historical interpretation are avoided, but a conscious effort is made to subordinate them to concrete ones such as how to choose a subject, how to use a library, how to take notes, when to quote, when to use a footnote, how to evaluate evidence, how to tell a good work of history from a bad one, how to prepare a manuscript, and how to write a historical composition.

The available textbooks on historical method, despite their sometimes obvious merit, rarely meet the needs of students in a course of this nature. With some notable exceptions, they are not laboratory manuals. They deal too abstractly with the practical questions to which the beginning student wants answers. Instead of attempting to tell him what sort of notes are worth taking or when not to use a footnote or how to avoid irrelevance in historical narrative, they present overwhelming bibliographies or speak abstrusely about the detection of unauthentic manuscripts and about the sciences auxiliary to history. In a day when nearly any American college library has printed and manuscript collections of well authenticated and well catalogued documents, these techniques are rarely so important as they once were when the student had to learn how to compile his own collections or so important as they will become when the student goes beyond the walls of his college library to work in less systematic collections and archives. Nor do the available textbooks on historical method often deal with problems of style (except perhaps at the hortatory level); and when they raise questions dealing with the relations of history to the social sciences and philosophy or with the possibilities of generalization, prediction, and control in history, they are apt to do so in a rarefied, academic atmosphere.

Yet any of these questions may arise as practical questions in the course of preparing a historical composition. History is three-dimensional. It partakes of the nature of science, art, and philosophy. As a method, it follows strict rules for ascertaining verifiable fact; as exposition and narrative, it calls for imagination, literary taste, and critical standards; as interpretation of life, it demands the philosopher's insights and judgments. The books generally available to the beginner deal so largely with method alone that they rarely mention the theory of history or its literary dimension. An attempt has been made here to discuss practice, style, and theory in an elementary fashion, and in the order in which they might become uppermost in the inexpert historian's mind (though they might easily arise simultaneously). Beginning with a brief discussion of the nature of history, we move on to a consideration of historical method and then to some remarks on the problem of style, ending with a discussion of some theoretical questions. While I have had the student of history primarily in mind, I have not tried to hide that the historian has to face these questions at every level in a world that is becoming more and more indifferent to *historia historiae gratia*. These are no longer merely academic questions or dimly felt annoyances on the periphery of a genteel profession. The answers may well determine not only how genteel the profession may remain but whether it ought in fact to be suffered to exist as an independent discipline.

To questions as intricate and moot as some of these it would be folly to claim to have the right answers. I would feel flattered if I could persuade myself that even those of my colleagues to whom this book is dedicated shared my belief in their correctness. If my answers appear false to any reader, the fault is mine alone. I hope, however, that readers will believe them at least worthy of consideration as points of departure for further discussion. For that reason I thought it desirable not merely to describe practices that I consider generally accepted among historians but also to make proposals (sometimes already made by others) that may prove widely acceptable, and have tried to make clear the distinction between descriptive statements and proposals.

This work has been written primarily for the student of history in the colleges and universities. The needs of the independent general reader, not directly concerned with writing history himself but wishing to acquire standards of judging historical writing, have also been constantly kept in mind. It has been assumed throughout that the reader has profounder love than knowledge of history but sufficient knowledge to manage without a trained guide. If this assumption has led occasionally to elaboration of the obvious on the one hand and oversimplification of the complex on the other, it is intentionally so. This work is addressed to the beginner and the amateur. The more advanced reader may find it desirable to skip Chapters III–VII, and perhaps teachers of historical method should begin with Chapter VIII.

LOUIS GOTTSCHALK

ACKNOWLEDGMENTS

Chapters II, III, V, VI, VII, IX, X, and XI of this book have drawn heavily upon my essay entitled "The Historian and the Historical Document" in The Use of Personal Documents in History, Anthropology and Sociology *(New York: Social Science Research Council Bulletin No. 53, 1945). I am greatly indebted to the Social Science Research Council for permission to repeat or to rework almost all of that essay in this book. I am also indebted to the Social Science Research Council for allowing me to quote from its Bulletin No. 54,* Theory and Practice in Historical Study: a Report of the Committee on Historiography *(New York, 1946) and from W. I. Thomas and Florian Znaniecki,* The Polish Peasant in Europe and America *(Boston, 1918–20). I was a member of the Committee on Historiography and profited from its meetings (in more ways than can be guessed merely by my references to its report) as well as from public and private comments upon that report. Chapter I has been derived largely from my essay entitled "The Evaluation of Historical Writings" in Louis Wilson (ed.),* The Practice of Book Selection *(Chicago, 1940), which the University of Chicago Press has kindly permitted me to adapt to the needs of this book. Only Chapters IV and VIII appear here entirely for the first time, but all chapters have in them much that is new.*

I am also indebted to Doubleday & Co. and Charles Scribner's Sons for permission to quote from works which they have published. To Bruce L. Smith and the Gradu-

ate Library School of the University of Chicago I owe information about technological improvements in bibliographical work. Quincy Wright has allowed me to use some lines from one of his speeches, and Vincent Starrett and Marya Mannes to quote in full a little poem of each. I owe the whole of the Appendix to Raymond Preston. I shall acknowledge my indebtedness again in the footnotes to these borrowed passages.

Where I have wanted to illustrate a point with an example, I have not hesitated to invent one that I thought was representative, but in a number of instances I have borrowed without acknowledgment from papers by students under my supervision. The illustrations that I have thus unceremoniously appropriated, it will be noted, are not always of horrible examples to avoid. This is perhaps the place to acknowledge my great debt to the many able young men and women who in "History 300 or its equivalent" and "History 408 or its equivalent" have contributed, among other things, to my training in how to teach historical method at least as much as I have contributed to their learning it.

Several friends have helped me to prepare this work. They have been loyally and intelligently severe in their criticism. I should like to thank especially James L. Cate, Fruma Gottschalk, William T. Hutchinson, and Margaret Maddox, all of whom made corrections and suggestions at some stage before the manuscript went to press and caused me to eliminate certain weaknesses. If the book still has shortcomings, they are probably more attributable to my persistence than to any oversight on the part of these friendly critics.

CONTENTS

PART ONE
OBJECTIVES OF HISTORIANS

PART TWO

METHODS OF HISTORICAL RESEARCH

PART THREE

THEORY OF HISTORY

PART ONE

Objectives of Historians

CHAPTER I

THE EVALUATION
OF HISTORICAL WRITING[1]

History and Patriotism

AT times of national crisis, such as war or periods of post-war readjustment, historians are likely to find themselves under pressure to sentimentalize the story of their country's development — if necessary, with some disregard of the truth. The teaching of history can indeed be used for the training of loyal citizens if the story of one's country is truly one of which the patriot can be proud or if it can be so modified and manipulated as to make it seem elevating. That, at least in part, explains why Napoleon Bonaparte preferred to suppress the "moral sciences" in the Institute, why the Nazis claimed a predominant German influence in America for the good and a predominant Jewish influence in Germany for the bad, and why the Stalinists have resurrected some significant Russian heroes. Dictators and the cruder variety of democratic politicians prefer to think of history not as a branch of knowledge with its own method for attaining verisimilitude but as a means toward achieving that brand of patriotism that can be based upon an uncritical examination of their country's history.

---

[1] Adapted from the author's article by the same title in Louis Wilson (ed.), *The Practice of Book Selection* (Chicago: University of Chicago Press, 1940), pp. 101–15.

Upon the close of the First World War, the ancient controversy sharply divided American historians from politicians, with a citizen of Chicago among the chief protagonists of each school. Andrew C. McLaughlin, of whom perhaps Mayor William Hale Thompson had rarely heard, was among those attacked for their interpretation of American history by the very audible mayor, whom or of whom everybody had heard. The issue was whether our schoolbooks were sufficiently patriotic, and "Big Bill" Thompson, who apparently had only recently learned of King George III of England, wanted to "poke him in the nose," and complained to all and sundry because the textbooks used in our secondary schools painted his erstwhile majesty as possessed of almost human attributes. In those days of Lusk "loyalty" committees, Palmer "Red" raids, and daily prognostications of Soviet Russia's collapse, it was no hard task for Thompson to win followers; and historians who wrote telling essays decrying certain types of patriotism as the last refuge of scoundrels had to be content with holding each other's hands. Textbooks written in the next decade or so were sometimes revised at the suggestion of publishers in order to avoid the displeasure of patrioteers on the school boards of our major cities.

As war hysteria and the Red scare subsided, academic detachment was allowed to creep back into our schoolbooks. All would have gone well, and history might have descended to an all too natural level of gravedigging for the idly curious, had it not been for the Black and Brown scares that in the 1930's came to replace the panic of the twenties. Some very serious and scholarly gentlemen then began to feel that pure historical scholarship was a danger. It enabled historians in a democracy, who were free, to dig up the dirt around their great national heroes at the very moment when any unpleasant truths about the great figures of the totalitarian states were being most carefully suppressed. It made a reverential attitude toward the ideals and the idealists of the democratic past seem outmoded at the very time that democracy was most in need of idealism in its struggle against the forces of totalitarianism.

Learned articles eloquently urged that historians respect the odor of sanctity that surrounds our great men.[2] They deplored the modern textbook's tendency to be silent regarding the noble declarations of which our wise ancestors are said to have calmly delivered themselves at the most crucial moments of our past. This campaign for a national mythology was joined by several competent journalists. They recognized the danger of misrepresentation, but they felt that the risk must be run.

Nevertheless, patriotism as a norm for the evaluation of historical writings must always be suspect to the critical reader. That is not only because there is small likelihood of agreement among equally convinced patriots regarding what is patriotic. Catholic martyrs, for example, are not likely to appear equally holy to Protestants; German heroes may appear somewhat less than heroic to Frenchmen; Republican titans appear to Democrats to be of fairly average size; and

[2] Cf. H. M. Jones, "Patriotism — But How?" *Atlantic Monthly*, November, 1938, pp. 585–92.

there is frequently legitimate ground for dispute as to whose nationals first made some important invention. It is also due to the fact that of the making of saints there can be no end.

An example of how ardor may lead even an intelligent and critical writer into error appeared in an editorial in the *Chicago Daily News* in the midst of a recent journalistic campaign for a more patriotic American history.[3] The writer, anxious to show that historians have been over-iconoclastic, maintained that it was perfectly possible for Washington, while crossing the ice-filled Delaware in an overcrowded rowboat, to have stood up and grasped the American flag, as the well-known portrait of Emanuel Leutze shows him doing. The argument is an excellent one, but it is beside the point. The reason for questioning the historicity of Leutze's picture is not that Washington is shown standing up. Skepticism arises rather from the fact that the flag he is pictured clutching in his protecting hand is the Stars and Stripes, which was adopted by Congress as the flag of the United States only on June 4, 1777, and probably was not in use before that date. In other words, Maestro Leutze, had been not only patriotic but also anachronistic. To assign patriotism a place superior to historical truth may be a becoming gradation of virtues in a painter and even in a journalist, but not in the historian *qua* historian.

---

[3] Royal F. Munger, "Old Bill Suggests," January 6, 1939. See also the editorial, ibid., January 4, 1939.

History and the Democratic Faith

In all fairness to the patriotic company, it should be pointed out that they were concerned more with the problem of adolescent education than with research. Yet even in adolescent education, when the truth can be determined by historical methods, perhaps it should be presented unvarnished. A patriotism which rests on historical legends cannot be a lasting patriotism. No patriot serves his country well who hides the clay feet of his country's idols beneath layers of gilt. It is far wiser to let children see the clay, the better to appreciate the few pieces of Parian marble and genuine gold that the idols may contain. The children would be less likely ever to become disillusioned, as did the generation of whose indifference to our national myths these critics complained.

A better and more lasting patriotism can be inculcated by a frank and unabashed preaching of democratic ideals as a faith. Few think any the less of Judaism because Moses killed a man; or of Catholicism because Augustine was a sinner in his younger days; or of Protestantism because Calvin had Servetus burned at the stake. If we hold with religious fervor to our democratic ideals of liberty of expression, equality of opportunity, and tolerance of others' creeds and opinions, what difference will it make that some of democracy's heroes were land-grabbers, job-hunters, and publicity hounds? Our ideals, not a series of frail mortals, ought to be held up to our school children as the foundation of our national creed. The problem is a pedagogical, not a research problem.

Is History Art or Science?

Yet faith is not altogether alien to history. In his presidential address to the American Historical Association in 1933, which he entitled "Written History as an Act of Faith," [4] Charles A. Beard maintained that they complement each other. History is, to be sure, scientific in method; millions of historical facts can be established as convincingly for laymen and experts alike as that two and two make four or that hydrogen and oxygen mixed in certain proportions under certain conditions make water. There can be no doubt, for example, that on a day conveniently labeled "October 12, 1492," a group of sailors captained by a man known in English as "Christopher Columbus" landed on an island which was apparently the one now called "Watling Island." The truth of that event is proved by a series of documents so carefully tested for authenticity and credibility that, until more authentic and more credible documents are discovered which would call it in question, the historian considers it a fact, or more accurately a series of facts, and the layman doubts it no more than he does the multiplication table. There are a myriad of similar facts equally scientifically established for both historian and layman. They are the unfinished materials of history.

Making such unfinished materials into a book, however, requires that they be selected, arranged, and described or narrated. These processes we have called *historiography* and have distinguished from analytical historical method (pp. 48–9). Historical method is,

[4] *American Historical Review*, XXXIX (1934), 219–31.

within limits, scientific — i.e., its results are subject to verification and to intelligent agreement or disagreement among the experts. Historiography is more likely to be art, philosophy, polemic, propaganda, or special pleading. Sometimes the historian is consciously a pointer of morals; sometimes he is unconsciously so. It is when he is unaware that he has a philosophy, or more particularly when he thinks he has a philosophy which in fact he does not have, that he is dangerous. An intellectually honest writer who realizes that he is a liberal or conservative, Protestant or Catholic, American or German, white or black, middle-class or proletarian, either can lean over backward against his predilections in order to achieve a greater degree of impartiality or can inform his readers of his predilections so that they may be forewarned against them — or, preferably, he can do both. The writer who thinks he has no philosophy of history or who believes he is detached is self-deceived, unless he is more than human, and therefore more likely to deceive others than if he were deliberately lying. Whenever historians defend the scientific objectivity of history,[5] they are most likely to have in mind the historian's ability to prove single facts or sequences of fact. Unless they insist that their own interpretations are the only possible correct ones, they cannot maintain that there can be much more than a sweet reasonableness in their evaluation, selection, emphasis, and arrangement of those facts or sequences. The amazing thing, since so many variables enter into historical judgments, is not that

---

[5] Cf. C. H. McIlwain, "The Historians' Part in a Changing World," ibid., XLII (1937), 207–24.

historians disagree but that they agree as often as they do.

History, Philosophy, and Ethics

For the very reason that there are so many variables in the presentation of historical data, truth ceases to be the only criterion for judging the value of historical writings. Second on a list of norms for their evaluation would come the intelligence of the writer's philosophical principles. The historian cannot avoid, and therefore it is better that he should be openly committed to, some philosophy and some code of ethics. He should know whether he is a materialist or an idealist, a liberal or a conservative, a religious skeptic or a devotee, a believer in the progress or in the imperfectibility of mankind, in the psychoanalytic or the psychosomatic, the economic or the technological, the geographical or the climatological, the epistemological or the providential theory of historical interpretation, or in any combination or permutation of these philosophical and ethical principles, and many more like them. Furthermore, the historian who has no philosophical or ethical principles has no criteria for measuring change or continuity and therefore cannot judge development, rise, fall, growth, stagnation, decay, fertility, or sterility. Without such judgments historical writing cannot be good narrative or description, which are the essence of history. Where there is no sense of development, there can be a cataloguing of details in chronological order or under some logical system of subheadings, but there cannot be presented a running story of genesis, growth, stability, stagnation, or decay. And to tell whether things grow or decay, or merely continue or recur without growing or decaying, one must have some idea of what growth is. That means a philosophy of ends and a standard of good and bad.

The greatest historians of the past had such philosophies and standards. Thucydides, Tacitus, Voltaire, Gibbon, Macaulay, wrote for a purpose with definite standards of judgment. To evaluate their standards, one must have standards of one's own. One cannot say that their standards are objectively true or false; one can only say that they appeal as intelligent or unintelligent, appear right or wrong in the light of one's own criteria. In short, not only to write history that will be more than a mere cataloguing of facts but also in order to judge the historical writings of others intelligently, the historian needs some philosophical and ethical rules.

There will presumably be vast room for differences of opinion regarding the intelligence of these rules. Moreover, that room does not necessarily diminish with the more extensive reading of historical classics. Justice, truth, beauty, godliness, generosity, tolerance, optimism, progress, philanthropy, liberty, equality, peace, patriotism, good sportsmanship, efficiency, health, law and order — all these may be intelligent philosophical and ethical principles and have been championed by some historians at some time in the past. They are not, however, either exhaustive of all intelligent criteria or necessarily mutually consistent. Besides, historians occasionally have championed tolerance intolerantly, philanthropy with misanthropic bitterness, equality with an unconcealed sense of superiority, and often with a monistic emphasis which alone would lead their readers to skepticism, just as philosophers, in the words of one of them, occasionally have loved the world in order to avoid loving their neighbors. Assuredly less likelihood exists that historians will agree regarding their philosophical and ethical principles than regarding the truth of the materials which they must interpret in the light of these principles. Until that far-distant era of philosophical harmony, historians must be tolerant of one another, asking only that their principles be not too conspicuously of transient value, too obviously *ad hoc*, too patently for ulterior motives.

Mutual tolerance may seem like passively marking time in the presence of horrible danger to the historians' social and intellectual values. But those who clamor loudly for more vigorous measures and greater unity of purpose among the historians seem unlikely to be able to propose a set of principles upon which all can agree. Faith in the ultimate triumphs of liberty and respect for democracy's martyrs would seem to be axiomatic for the historians of the West, but the historians of totalitarian states would consider such a faith simple, shallow, and time-serving. They, like the historians of the Middle Ages, have a distinct advantage over the rest of us; their ethical and philosophical principles are dictated for them, and to admit of any others or to question the validity of those dictated is heresy. They have unity of purpose, yet it cannot be said that they have written better books than the historians of the democracies. Perhaps the explanation of that paradox is that philosophical principles ought not to be learned by rote but ought to be derived from and to coincide with one's experience. If Augustine wrote more influential books than the naive historian Agnellus, though their underlying philosophies were similar, perhaps it was in some part because Augustine acquired his philosophy and Agnellus had his thrust upon him — or at best was born to it and accepted it without reflection.

History and Literary Style

It must also be pointed out that Augustine knew how to write better than Agnellus. And that raises the question of literary merit in historical writing. Well-meaning critics have written some deserved tirades against the pedestrian style of academic historians.[6] The elephantine pace of many a historian's prose is often a direct outcome of a straining for accuracy of detail and precision of the whole at the express sacrifice of felicity. Commendable though such a deliberate choice may sometimes be, it is frequently doubtful whether it is justifiable. For the very dullness of style may in itself be a means of creating misapprehension. It is not easy to conceive of a historical episode that was not intensely interesting to someone, even when — like exile, imprisonment, illness, or monotonous labor — it might have had its full quota of boredom, perhaps for the same person. To represent historical episodes with a uniform dullness is thus, at least in part, to misrepresent them.

---

[6] Cf. Allan Nevins, "What's the Matter with History?" *Saturday Review of Literature*, February 4, 1939, pp. 3–4 and 16.

In fact, the historian who writes uninterestingly is to that extent a bad historian. He is professionally under obligation to describe, along with the ordinary, the most exciting events of the world's past and to re-create their atmosphere. If his account of a battle reads like a gunsmith's catalogue, if his tale of a hero's romance sounds like a license clerk's register, he is failing to reconstruct the proper atmosphere. Too many so-called history books succeed in bogging down battles, romances, discoveries, revolutions, frontier struggles, booms and depressions, industrial conflicts, intellectual triumphs, and national rejoicings in the same slough of uninspired verbiage. Even monotony and boredom can be eloquently described, and it is doubtful that a drab description of them — especially when the drabness is unintentional — would be more truthful than an eloquent one. A reference to any dictionary of quotations under "Boredom" or "Monotony" should carry conviction on that score.

It is probably true that those whose observations are memorialized in dictionaries of quotations seldom have had to work with bibliographies, reference works, archives, collections of documents, stacks of notes, and cross references. They have probably seldom had to bear the burden of the injunction to commit themselves definitely to no statement that was not supported by the independent testimony of two reliable witnesses or otherwise confirmed. Their imagination and their talents for self-expression have probably rarely been cramped by a due regard for footnotes and the canons of historical method. It must be admitted that a proper respect for historical accuracy may act as a checkrein upon the spirited pen. But the critics of the academic historian's style do not expect him to write like Voltaire, Schiller, Macaulay, or Henry Adams. They want him merely to write simply, to avoid irrelevancies and pedantries, and to know enough about style to permit his prose to be a vehicle for, rather than an impediment to, the intrinsic interest of the things he tells.

That kind of style can be learned. It is partly a result of effort — of writing, revising, and rewriting — and partly a result of growing up. A comparison of the early with the later writings of many historians now generally conceded to be good stylists would seem to demonstrate the telling rôle of mere industry and experience in the improvement of literary quality. Stylistic skill can be learned by continued application, and accumulative experience gives greater understanding of human behavior. History is life; he who has not lived, or has lived only enough to write a doctoral dissertation, is too inexperienced with life to write good history. He knows too little of the motives and associations of human beings, of love, hate, war, peace, inflation, ambition, sacrifice, suffering, fear, poverty, prosperity, revolution, propaganda, intolerance, boredom, frustration, and struggle to transfer his experience to paper. For the historian is different from the reader of novels. Instead of living vicariously the lives of his characters, to a large extent he makes his characters live his life, since he can understand them only by analogy, comparison, or contrast with his own experience.

Other things being equal, the historian who has experienced the most is the best historian. That does not mean the historian who has led the most adventurous life. Some can come closer to an understanding of their fellowmen sitting in an armchair with a book of poems as an only companion than others can in years of front-line soldiering. The imaginative spirit has no need to burn cities or impale newborn babies in order to understand hate, fear, and suffering. Yet even the artist born understands better as he grows older. The poet's admonition to the poet speaks to the historian as well:

> If poets are not listened to, the blame
> Is theirs. They speak unclearly and are lost
> In their own psychic maze and the intricate game
> Of words. In a twisted world what matters most
> Is simple statement open to the least
> Of men. No precious patterns hold the ear
> Nor can the chaotic spirit be released
> By further chaos. Those in doubt and fear
> Lean to the sure and fearless. Now to be heard
> The poet must speak plainly. The obscure
> Is powerless over violence. Each word
> Must be inevitable, urgent, pure,
> If people are to hear, above the roar,
> The voice of those who know what speech is for.[7]

---

[7] Quoted by permission of the author, Marya Mannes. An interesting example of unintentional historical misrepresentation occurs in connection with this poem. It was included by error in the posthumous work of James Boyd, *Eighteen Poems* (New York: Scribner, 1944), and its true authorship was not discovered until after publication.

Good Style and Good Scholarship

The problem of style can be solved, in part, by cooperative effort. After the painstaking historian has set down carefully the story he has extracted from the sources, an editor or a collaborator with a literary flair might "re-write" it. Where the two authors are well teamed, such an arrangement may sometimes be desirable. The danger lies in the possibility that the "re-write" man may prefer popular writing to good history. He might be able to give to a serious historical effort more zest or refinement only at the risk of accuracy of expression. A re-write man would scarcely let stand, for example, the sentence above (p. 8): "On a day conveniently labeled 'October 12, 1492,' a group of sailors captained by a man known in English as 'Christopher Columbus' landed on an island which was apparently the one now called 'Watling Island.'" He would probably translate it into something like: "Columbus discovered America on October 12, 1492." But that is exactly what a historian with an eye for accuracy rather than style might wish to avoid saying. The more wordy phrasing of the same thought was deliberate. It was due to awareness of other methods of dating than the Gregorian calendar; to doubts regarding whether Columbus was the first of his men to step on American soil; to contentions that others had reached America before Columbus' men; to conflicts regarding the nationality of Columbus; to arguments that a man who reaches a remote island cannot lay claim to the discovery of a continent; and to uncertainty regarding the particular island on which he did land. A re-write man might encounter too much difficulty if he tried to get all of those doubts and conflicts into a "zippy" sentence.

The serious writer sometimes finds himself faced with the obligation to choose between accurate history and popularity. For the scholar, in such a dilemma, the choice is easy: distorting history is a greater offense than torpid writing.[8] The argument that such a scale of values reduces scholars to writing for each other may be true but should not carry too much weight with those who have any use for scholarship at all. If a writer's object is to sell books or articles rather than to improve the knowledge and interpretation of history, he should choose a subject so popular to begin with that nearly all the necessary research has already been done by experts and all that remains to be done is to present it for popular approval. Such popularization can well be left to competent hacks with a literary flair. That, however, does not excuse the scholarly historian either from cultivating a lively style or from responsibility for the popularization of his subject. If history is to remain the living past, serious historical scholarship must not be still-born.

The choice between accuracy and pithy statement is not the only choice the historian struggling for literary quality has to make. He must also choose between a pose of omniscience and an argumentative style. The pose of omniscience will prompt him to state positively what no one really knows; it will embolden him to give as facts what are only surmises.

[8] Cf. Bernard De Voto, "What's the Matter with History?" *Harper's Magazine*, CLXXIX (1939), 110.

By means of such omniscience Emil Ludwig informs us what went on in Napoleon's mind and Lytton Strachey what went on in Victoria's heart. If either had stopped to say: "This is what I think went on in the mind or heart for such and such reasons," he would not only have had to argue instead of assert but he would also have had to bolster his argument with footnotes; and few things will so thoroughly interfere with book sales as footnotes.

The Use of Footnotes

And yet footnotes have their uses. The historian who dispenses with them in a serious work dispenses with one of the means whereby others may test his conclusions. Footnotes enable the intelligent reader to know *how* the writer knows; and for the historian — as historian rather than as the purveyor of bread and shoes to his family — one intelligent reader is worth more than a hundred of the kind that frequently crowd into book clubs. Moreover, the footnote enables the discriminating writer to secure greater accuracy. If Ludwig had not avoided footnotes as the plague, he might have discovered that he was citing Napoleon's letters out of all chronological and logical order. Or perhaps he knew that but preferred "zip" at any price.

The most justifiable reason for using a footnote to a narrative or expository text is to indicate the source of a statement that is challengeable. The footnote thus takes the place of the summons to a witness in a court of law. It is preferably as brief as possible. Sometimes, where witnesses disagree, it may be necessary to call several of them — i.e., to indicate their disagreement and even to resolve the differences between them in a footnote. In that case, the footnote may become fairly lengthy, but it will still be exclusively for the purpose of documentation, showing the source of the testimony upon which the footnoted statement or statements rest. It has also become conventional to footnote quotations or paraphrases from the sources. These practices fulfill the useful purpose of allowing the specialist or the interested reader to verify the challengeable statement or the quoted words for himself and of providing the future investigators of related subjects with bibliographical leads. If they are succinct and businesslike, there can be little objection to them, particularly since a set of abbreviations has been developed that enables the scholar to use a conventional shorthand for the identification of titles used a second time or more. The reader who is not interested in challenge, verification, or further investigation is not called upon to pay any attention to them.

The Abuse of Footnotes

The popular dislike of footnotes arises from the slovenliness or the pedantry of authors. Pedantic footnotes are frequently of the sort that will be discussed later (p. 200) — comments of doubtful relevance to the text that the author could not bring himself to excise entirely. Sometimes they contain identification of persons and things mentioned in the text by an author who has not been skillful enough to identify them as he wrote. This criticism would not apply to the editing of a document in its original form. In such cases, the footnote is expressly used for purposes of identification. Documents, however, are intended for other scholars; they are not prepared with the general reader in mind. Footnotes that result from the author's lack of literary skill are more pardonable than those that result from sheer pedantry. Outstanding among these is the footnote that unnecessarily displays the author's bibliographical equipment or his knowledge of foreign languages. Worst of all are the footnotes that reveal slovenliness; they are the patent insertions resulting from new information that has come to the author's attention after completion of his manuscript and that the pressure of time or, more often, the author's reluctance has not permitted him to incorporate smoothly into his text. Of course, where new testimony becomes available only after a work is already in the press, such footnotes are forgivable.

Footnotes that are more than summonses to witnesses cannot be disregarded by the general reader, for they may (though they frequently do not) contain something important to the understanding of the text. Thus, because historians have rarely learned to write footnotes chiefly for the specialist, the general public has never been trained to disregard them; and since they frequently are annoying, the general public has developed a prejudice against them. Perhaps it is not yet too late to counteract this prejudice by the studious avoidance of pedantic and slovenly footnotes.

History and Popular Taste

What makes a book popular? Is it because it is well written? In part, but the principal consideration perhaps is not so much "How well written?" as "About what or whom?" A biographical study, for example, that takes its subject from birth to death will probably have more general appeal than one that deals with only a critical period of his life. In the United States, it is probably a safe guess, a life of Washington, Lincoln, or Franklin Roosevelt, no matter how unoriginal, will outstrip in sales almost any life of Julius Caesar, Charlemagne, William the Silent, Napoleon, or Cavour, no matter how reinterpretative; and lives of major figures will have a better chance to succeed than biographies of minor ones, whether national or foreign. In the same general way, historical narratives other than biographies may also be measured for probable success. Works of history dealing with the United States or with a timely topic will sell in America, other things being equal, better than works dealing with a European, a minor country, or a remote topic. A similar preference for national heroes and the national history would be found in other countries as well.

This quite natural preference perhaps explains why some beautifully written books, with or without footnotes, when they deal with a foreign country in a remote age, have failed to find a market. A book is not necessarily inferior either as history or as literature merely because all the persons mentioned in it were foreigners who have long been dead. The writing of history might soon be largely limited to national or to recent events — or, at best, to outstanding names and episodes — if it dealt only with what had popular appeal. As the list of annual prize awards and best sellers too often reveals, to be guided by popular taste means to run the risk of limiting historical literature not only to low literary standards but also to a few highly restricted fields of attention, such as the recent, the timely, the sensational, the classic, the exotic, the erotic, and the patriotic.

The Obligation of the Book Reviewer

The cure for the low literary quality of historical writing may be popular history magazines, as has sometimes been suggested. Commendable though such magazines may be, however, they will do little to raise the general literary level of historical output so long as other channels remain open for shoddy work. Nor does it help the flow of a dried-up stream to widen its outlet. The answer lies rather in a reduction of the amount of bad historical writing that gets published.

Perhaps the only way to eliminate the many dull, pedantic, inaccurate, petty, or useless works of history that every year clutter the market would be through higher and franker standards of historical criticism. Book publishers pay competent experts to evaluate manuscripts before accepting them for publication. The publishers ask such questions as: What does the author intend to do (since it is obviously unfair to criticize him for not doing something he did not set out to do)? How well did he do it? If it is well done, who can be expected to buy it? Will it have to compete with other books on the subject, and if so, what chance does it have of doing so successfully? If reviewers of published books were asked and expected to answer equally searching questions by book review editors, we might have higher standards of book reviewing.

Five questions for serious book reviewers (and readers in general) to ask of a book seem inescapable:

1. Does it establish its factual details by a strict application of the historical method?

2. Does it have a philosophy or "frame of reference" that is of more than transient and local significance and of more than private validity?

3. Is it written in a style that helps rather than impedes the reader's understanding?

4. Is it merely a piece of hackwork repeating an already known story, or does it present new data or new interpretation of old data?

5. No matter how limited its subject may be, does the author seem aware of the questions that men at all times in all places persist in asking?

Historiography has been defined as "taking little bits out of a great many books which no one has ever read and putting them together into one book which no one will read." It is not inconceivable that in the category of books "which no one has ever read" are some excellent though neglected ones. Moreover, the historian would like to keep some copies of them all for the sake of record. Perhaps, therefore, nothing should be done to diminish the number of works already in existence which no one does or should read, but it behooves those who read, write, and especially review historical work to do what they can to diminish the rate of increase of new ones. It may then develop that more talent and money will become available for works that can meet the higher standards.

CHAPTER II

THE RELATION OF HISTORICAL
METHOD TO LIFE AND LEARNING

"Every Man His Own Historian"

EVERY normal adult knows, has read, and has written enough history to find pat illustrations of most of the problems with which this book deals. The normal adult has a memory that embraces several years of experience. In the course of that experience he has read and heard many historical documents — among them newspapers, letters, public and legal papers, radio announcements, political speeches, official statistics, advertisements, and ordinary conversations. He has also written many potential historical documents — school exercises, tax reports, personal and business letters, speeches, notes in notebooks or on scraps of paper, comments in the margins of the books he has read, expense accounts, household budgets, journal and ledger entries, bills and orders at the stores, minutes of his club, score cards, datebook and diary entries, and so on. Any one of these, if it should fall into the hands of a historian interested in him, or the place in which he lived, or his times, or the activities in which he engaged, might become a source of some knowledge, no matter how meager and unreliable. The people who threw away old household and business accounts in ancient Egypt thousands of years ago probably had no thought of today's historian. Nevertheless, from their old scraps of paper (or, more accurately, papyrus) scholars now learn much that might otherwise remain unknown about the households, institutions, business methods, prices, and everyday life of a vanished age. The name of an obscure scribe or of a lowly worker, if found upon a moldering papyrus, is recorded perhaps forever, but the names of mighty lords and great conquerors are lost beyond recall if they were nowhere recorded or if the record of them has disappeared. Every man is not only a historian having to compose, if only in his thoughts, his own history for his own understanding, but he also has a chance of being among those whose records will come to the attention of the historian several decades or millennia hence and so win an immortality that may be denied to his more prominent contemporaries.

The Essentials of Historical Method

Unless the methods of history undergo a greater change in the future than they have in the past, the historian of that future age will have to proceed in much the same way as is sketched in this book with regard to any historical documents that survive from our hands. Having found the documents, he will have to establish two things about them: first, are they authentic, or which parts of them are, if only some of them or sections of some of them are authentic? second, how much of the authentic parts are credible, and to what an extent? That is all he will be able to learn from the documents themselves. Merely finding and authenticating the documents, however, or even editing them critically with shrewd indications of their credibility, will make him only a specialist engaged in work auxiliary to history. If he is going to be a historian of us and our times, a harder problem will face him. That will be how to put together the details he has reliably learned from the authentic documents into a connected narrative or exposition. When he has done those three things and only when he has done all three, will he have become a historian (no matter how inadequately) of us and our times.

Thus how to write history of any particular place, period, and set of events, institutions, or persons reduces itself to four bare essentials:

1. the collection of the surviving objects and of the printed, written, and oral materials that may be relevant;

2. the exclusion of those materials (or parts thereof) that are unauthentic;

3. the extraction from the authentic material of testimony that is credible;

4. the organization of that reliable testimony into a meaningful narrative or exposition. An understanding of those four steps, and a set of standards of competence for each of them, are required for the intelligent reading of what historians have written. This book is concerned with the exposition of those four steps.

The Constancy of the Historical Method

History has been variously considered a form of belles-lettres, a branch of the humanistic studies, a handmaiden of the social sciences, and a method for the better understanding of all the arts and sciences. Whether any, all, or none of these classifications is true makes no difference in the way the historian proceeds to analyze surviving testimony for reliable evidence about the past of mankind, though, as we shall soon see, it may make a difference as to what kinds of evidence he will seek and how he will put them together. This analytical procedure we shall call "the historical method."

The Universality of the Historical Method

Some have seen in this method the major, if not the only, significance of history. "History," said Charles Seignobos, "is not a science; it is a method (*procédé de connaissance*)." [1] By that he meant that the historical method may be applied to the subject matter of any discipline whatsoever as a means of ascertaining fact. That is true. Even in disciplines that seem remote from the usual interests of the historian, such as the natural sciences, the inquirer, by ascertaining what others did in the past, can sometimes shed light upon experiments that might be either repeated if promising or modified if sterile; and for other disciplines, such as law, theology, business, philosophy, literature, art, and the social sciences, knowledge of genesis, precedent, previous experience, historical setting, past analogies, and contrasting situations has an obvious value. Around two centuries ago the German critic Gotthold Ephraim Lessing declared: "Without history . . . we shall be in hourly danger of being deceived by ignorant braggarts, who not infrequently hail as a new discovery what men knew and believed many

[1] *Méthode historique appliquée aux sciences sociales* (Paris, 1901), p. 3.

thousands of years ago." [2] With history we may still be deceived, but we also have a chance to learn from past example. History, for one thing, is the recorded experience of the human race, and man can profit from experience in any field of knowledge.

Still, it is no less true that the historical method has a special significance for the historian. The historian (or other scholar acting *in loco historici*) applies the historical method to evidence that has survived from the past and from it accumulates whatever credible data he can. These data may be used by the philosopher, the political scientist, the sociologist, the literary critic, or the physicist to construct a history of thought, of political institutions, of social customs, of literature, or of physics. But they are also used by the historian to construct descriptions of past personalities and places, narratives of past events, expositions of past ideas, or syntheses of past periods and cultures.

History Related to Both the Humanities and the Social Sciences

These reconstructions, it is contended here, ought to be built according to certain rules. If these rules are applied, historians can be not only scientific in their method of extracting elementary data but they may also aim at a scientific procedure (within all too obvious limits) in putting the data together. This point is argued without in any way committing the author to the side of those who maintain in the age-old debate that history is or ought to be exclusively either a com-

---

[2] Quoted in Mathys Jolles, "Lessing's Conception of History," *Modern Philology*, XLIII (1946), 185.

panion of the humanities or of the social sciences. In his opinion it may be either or it may be both. History may partake of the nature of the social sciences, and it is to be hoped that as such it may improve. But it is also concerned with the past for the sake of the past, with the individual man and with the particular human exploit or line of development because men are interesting as men. If the historian who considers himself a guardian of the cultural heritage and an interpreter of human development also seeks to reach generalizations that appear to be valid and to provide credit to explanations of the development of contemporary events, thoughts, manners, and institutions, he is, by the extra effort, no less, and he may be more, a historian.[3] If he prefers not to make the extra effort, he may still be a good historian. The historian as social scientist and the historian as humanist, however, need not be two separate persons; they may easily be the same one. And the usefulness of that one to both the humanities and the social sciences would be greatly increased if he were not to act schizophrenically.

The Relation of the Humanities and the Social Sciences

For the difference between the humanities and the social sciences can easily be exaggerated. The proper subject of both is man as a cultural, intellectual, and

---

[3] Cf. Proposition I in Merle Curti *et al.*, *Theory and Practice in Historical Study: a Report of the Committee on Historiography* (New York: Social Science Research Council Bulletin #54, 1946), p. 134.

social animal. Both wish to find generalizations (though the social scientist is usually more interested in prediction and control than the humanist, and the humanist usually more interested in the unique — preferably the outstanding — example than the social scientist). Both are interested in the past, the present, and the future (though the humanist tends to emphasize the past and the social scientist the present and the future). Grimm's philological law of the correspondence of consonants is no less a scientific generalization than Vierkandt's sociological law on the succession of destructive and constructive phases in revolution or Gresham's economic law on the relation of good and bad money — nor is it without significance to the social scientist. In fact it is even more dependent upon expert observation than Vierkandt's and Gresham's laws and much less reminiscent of the street corner and the cracker barrel.

Those who refuse to admit the close kinship of the humanities and the social sciences are likely to be ignorant of much of the good social science that has been propounded in the past by the philosophers and belle-lettrists, or of the good sense that is today being propounded by social scientists. Neither humanists nor social scientists would dare to overlook the philosopher Herbert Spencer. If, however, he had by some chance become important before modern sociology first was "founded," many sociologists would today neglect him; and if he were writing now, many humanists would turn up their noses at him — only to write learned dissertations about him a few decades hence in an effort to answer the kind of questions that the sociologists would today be raising about him; whereas the sociologists of that future decade, having already begun to forget him, would be moving on to similar questions about some more nearly contemporary figure.

The Historian as Social Scientist

The fact that Spencer and other outstanding philosophical figures are equally important to humanist and social scientist — along with other facts — tends to the conclusion that the two kinds of scholars sometimes differ more in emphasis and tense than in subject matter and purpose. The humanist historian need not be, but can be, the social scientist of the past. He need not be, because there is enough interest in the past for its own sake, enough demand for the preservation of the cultural heritage — the experiences, thoughts, manners, customs, religions, institutions, personalities, literature, arts, music, science, and wisdom of the past — to justify the humanist who wishes to devote himself to unique examples, isolated areas, remote epochs, or specialized lines of development. But he can relate those examples, areas, epochs, and lines of development to broader concepts and social generalizations if he cares and dares to make the additional effort. Alcibiades might justifiably be treated only as a Greek general and politician, but he could also be studied as an example of military and political personality-types; the Children's Crusade might well be described only as the story of a pathetic event in the year 1212, but it could also be used to illustrate a number of concepts of child psychology, social behavior, and religious experience; the poetry of John Dryden yields satisfaction when examined only for scansion, vocabulary, or phrasing, but it can also be exploited as a source of the history of contemporary ideas and of the contemporary intellectual atmosphere or as a part of the continuous ideology of mankind.

Three Ways of Studying Human Achievement

To be sure, the humanist may consider two other approaches to his subject as preferable to that of the social scientist. He may wish to study the great works of literature, art, or music analytically and aesthetically. He may be a literary critic, and the dramas of Shakespeare, for example, may be of interest to him largely because of their internal structure, style, and wisdom, and such history as he includes in his study may be included only to provide a knowledge of their antecedents. Or he may be a specialist in the substantive history of dramatic arts, and they may interest him as illustrating an important development of the theater unrelated in his mind to the contemporary social setting. Either kind of interest is not only separately legitimate but also commendable in the humanist. Still, only by deliberate effort could he eschew the "sociological history" of Shakespeare. The social historian, if he were interested in Shakespearean dramas, would be less likely to concern himself with literary criticism and the history of the drama than what he might call the "situational interrelations," "the social psychology," "the climate of opinion," "the social ecology," or "the knowledge sociology" of Shakespeare and his times. That is to say, Shakespeare's plays would be for him a manifestation of the inter-action between a culture and a personality.

Yet, obviously, Shakespeare's dramatic principles and qualities and the development of the Elizabethan drama were to some extent part of the "sociology," the cultural background, of Shakespeare's plays (and vice versa). Hence, the separation of the three meth-ods of study of Shakespeare — they might be called "the critical-analytical," "the substantive-historical," and "the socio-cultural" — is to that extent artificial and finds justification only in the necessity of spe-cialization and efficient distribution of time for the purposes of study. The historian, however, if he means fully to understand the biography of Shakespeare or Shakespeare as a representative of Elizabethan cul-ture or Shakespeare as a representative of the world's literary development or Shakespeare in any other his-torical context should make use of all three methods; and to the extent that he fails to do so, to that extent he fails as a historian.

The three possible ways of studying Shakespeare's plays would also be valid for the study of important accomplishments in other fields. Newton's experi-ments, for example, could be studied as part of the cause-and-effect interrelations of seventeenth-century English society, or as part of the substantive history of science, or as a critical analysis of his contributions to scientific thought. Napoleon's battles could be stud-ied as an expression and a cause of European culture in the nineteenth century or as episodes in the sub-stantive history of warfare or by a critical analysis of the strategy and tactics of his separate battles. Textbooks of general history, as a matter of fact, used to stop to analyze the tactics and strategy (size of armies, distribution of troops, topography, logistics, objectives, etc.) of battles or the contents of treaties to the point where a reaction set in against the overemphasis upon military and diplomatic details. Today textbooks stop to analyze significant accomplishments in literature, music, art, philosophy, and science.

The Historian's Interest in All Three Ways

Since every individual may write his own history (and certainly he thinks of it often), he may do so in a fashion that is some combination of the three approaches described above — the total cultural or sociological, the specialized, and the analytical. If he is a college student, for example, he may think of himself as a product of all the factors that have gone into making his society and culture, or he may try to place himself in the substantive history of education, or he may attempt an evaluation of his work and personality in a critical and analytical fashion. Stop now to think about yourself in all three ways. Then you will appreciate more fully the tremendous difficulties facing the historian who undertakes to do all these things and more for whole nations or cultures. These difficulties explain why so many of his profession have only limited success. He is not therefore relieved of his obligations, but the difficulty inherent in his work would suggest either caution and modesty in his choice of subject or deliberate boldness and conscious willingness to face criticism. Either caution or boldness may be virtues if calculated; what cannot be forgiven is a blind rushing-in because the difficulties are not understood.

In the forthcoming pages modesty is constantly urged upon beginners. They are asked to think in terms of the simple, precise, and concrete historical problem. After all, one learns to lay bricks one at a time, but it would be unfortunate if the skilled bricklayer thought of the laying of bricks one upon the other as the objective of his skill and never learned to think of magnificent edifices.

PART TWO

Methods of
Historical Research

CHAPTER III

WHAT ARE "HISTORY" AND "HISTORICAL SOURCES"?

The Meaning of "History"

THE ENGLISH word *history* is derived from the Greek noun ἰστορία, meaning *learning*. As used by the Greek philosopher Aristotle, *history* meant a systematic account of a set of natural phenomena, whether or not chronological ordering was a factor in the account; and that usage, though rare, still prevails in English in the phrase *natural history*. In the course of time, however, the equivalent Latin word *scientia* (English, *science*) came to be used more regularly to designate non-chronological systematic accounts of natural phenomena; and the word *history* was reserved usually for accounts of phenomena (especially human affairs) in chronological order.

By its most common definition, the word *history* now means "the past of mankind." Compare the German word for *history — Geschichte*, which is derived from *geschehen*, meaning *to happen. Geschichte* is *that which has happened*. This meaning of the word *history* is often encountered in such overworked phrases as "all history teaches" or "the lessons of history."

It requires only a moment's reflection to recognize that in this sense history cannot be reconstructed. The past of mankind for the most part is beyond recall. Even those who are blessed with the best memories cannot re-create their own past, since in the life of all men there must be events, persons, words, thoughts, places, and fancies that made no impression at all at the time they occurred, or have since been forgotten. A *fortiori*, the experience of a generation long dead, most of whom left no records or whose records, if they exist, have never been disturbed by the historian's touch, is beyond the possibility of total recollection. The reconstruction of the total past of mankind, although it is the goal of historians, thus becomes a goal they know full well is unattainable.

"Objectivity" and "Subjectivity"

Sometimes objects like ruins, parchments, and coins survive from the past. Otherwise, the facts of history are derived from testimony and therefore are facts of meaning. They cannot be seen, felt, tasted, heard, or smelled. They may be said to be symbolic or representative of something that once was real, but they have no objective reality of their own. In other words, they exist only in the observer's or historian's mind (and thus may be called "subjective"). To be studied objectively (that is, with the intention of acquiring detached and truthful knowledge independent of one's personal reactions), a thing must first be an object; it must have an independent existence outside the human mind. Recollections, however, do not have existence outside the human mind; and most of history is based upon recollections — that is, written or spoken testimony.

A vulgar prejudice exists against "subjective" knowledge as inferior to "objective" knowledge, largely because the word "subjective" has also come to mean "illusory" or "based upon personal considerations," and hence either "untrue" or "biased." Knowledge may be acquired, however, by an impartial and judicially detached investigation of mental images, processes, concepts, and precepts that are one or more steps removed from objective reality. Impartiality and "objectivity," to be sure, may be more difficult to obtain from such data, and hence conclusions based upon them may be more debatable; but such data and conclusions, if true, are not necessarily inferior to other kinds of knowledge *per se*. The word *subjective* is not used here to imply disparagement of any sort, but it does imply the necessity for the application of special kinds of safeguards against error.

Artifacts as Sources of History

Only where relics of human happenings can be found — a potsherd, a coin, a ruin, a manuscript, a book, a portrait, a stamp, a piece of wreckage, a strand of hair, or other archeological or anthropological remains — do we have *objects* other than words that the historian can study. These objects, however, are never the happenings or the events themselves. If artifacts, they are the results of events; if written documents, they may be the results or the records of events. Whether artifacts or documents, they are raw materials out of which history may be written.

To be sure, certain historical truths can be derived immediately from such materials. The historian can discover that a piece of pottery was handwrought, that a building was made of mortared brick, that a manuscript was written in a cursive hand, that a painting was done in oils, that sanitary plumbing was known in an old city, and many other such data from direct observation of artifacts surviving from the past. But such facts, important though they are, are not the essence of the study of history. The historian deals with the dynamic or genetic (the becoming) as well as the static (the being or the become) and he aims at being interpretative (explaining *why* and *how* things happened and were interrelated) as well as descriptive (telling *what* happened, *when* and *where*, and *who* took part). Besides, such descriptive data as can be derived directly and immediately from surviving artifacts are only a small part of the periods to which they belong. A historical context can be given to them only if they can be placed in a human setting. That human beings lived in the brick building with sanitary plumbing, ate out of the handwrought pottery, and admired the oil painting that were mentioned above might perhaps easily be inferred. But the inference may just as easily be mistaken, for the building might have been a stable, the piece of pottery might have been from a roof-tile, the painting might have been a hidden-away relic with no admirers whatsoever; and an infinity of other suppositions is possible. Without further evidence the human context of these artifacts can never be recaptured with any degree of certainty.

Historical Knowledge Limited
by Incomplete Records

Unfortunately, for most of the past we not only have no further evidence of the human setting in which to place surviving artifacts; we do not even have the artifacts. Most human affairs happen without leaving vestiges or records of any kind behind them. The past, having happened, has perished forever with only occasional traces. To begin with, although the absolute number of historical writings is staggering, only a small part of what happened in the past was ever observed. A moment's reflection is sufficient to establish that fact. How much, for example, of what you do, say, or think is ever observed by anyone (including yourself)? Multiply your unobserved actions, thoughts, words, and physiological processes by 2,000,000,000, and you will get a rough estimate of the amount of unobserved happenings that go on in the world all the time. And only a part of what was observed in the past was remembered by those who observed it; only a part of what was remembered was recorded; only a part of what was recorded has survived; only a part of what has survived has come to the historians' attention; only a part of what has come to their attention is credible; only a part of what is credible has been grasped; and only a part of what has been grasped can be expounded or narrated by the historian. The whole history of the past (what has been called *history-as-actuality*) can be known to him only through the surviving record of it (*history-as-record*), and most of history-as-record is only the surviving part of the recorded part of the remembered part of the observed part of that whole. Even when the record of the past is derived directly from archeological or anthropological remains, they are yet only the scholars' selected parts of the discovered parts of the chance survivals from the total past.

In so far as the historian has an external object to study it is not the perished history that actually happened (history-as-actuality) but the surviving records of what happened (history-as-record). History can be told only from history-as-record; and history as told (*spoken-or-written-history*) is only the historians' expressed part of the understood part of the credible part of the discovered part of history-as-record. Before the past is set forth by the historian, it is likely to have gone through eight separate steps at each of which some of it has been lost; and there is no guarantee that what remains is the most important, the largest, the most valuable, the most representative, or the most enduring part. In other words the "object" that the historian studies is not only incomplete; it is markedly variable as records are lost or rediscovered.

History as the Subjective Process of Re-creation

From this probably inadequate remainder the historian must do what he can to restore the total past of mankind. He has no way of doing it but in terms of his own experience. That experience, however, has taught him (1) that yesterday was different from today in some ways as well as the same as today in others, and (2) that his own experience is both like and unlike other men's. It is not alone his own memories interpreted in the light of his own experience that he must try to apply to the understanding of historical survivals; it is the memories of many other people as well. But one's own memories are abstract images, not realities, and one's reconstructions of others' memories, even when reinforced by contemporary records and relics, are likely to be even more abstract. Thus the utmost the historian can grasp of history-as-actuality, no matter how real it may have seemed while it was happening, can be nothing more than a mental image or a series of mental images based upon an application of his own experience, real and vicarious, to part of a part of a part of a part of a part of a part of a part of a part of a vanished whole.

In short, the historian's aim is *verisimilitude* with regard to a perished past — a subjective process — rather than experimental certainty with regard to an objective reality. He tries to get as close an approximation to the truth about the past as constant correction of his mental images will allow, at the same time recognizing that that truth has in fact eluded him forever. Here is the essential difference between the study of man's past and of man's physical environment. Physics, for example, has an extrinsic and whole object to study — the physical universe — that does not change because the physicist is studying it, no matter how much his understanding of it may change; history has only detached and scattered objects to study (documents and relics) that do not together

make up the total object that the historian is studying — the past of mankind — and that object, having
largely disappeared, exists only in as far as his always
incomplete and frequently changing understanding
of it can re-create it. Some of the natural scientists,
such as geologists and paleozoologists, in so far as the
objects they study are traces from a perished past,
greatly resemble historians in this regard, but differ
from them, on the other hand, in so far as historians
have to deal with human testimony as well as physical
traces.

Once the historian understands his predicament,
his task is simplified. His responsibility shifts from
the obligation to acquire a complete knowledge of
the irrecoverable past by means of the surviving evidence to that of re-creating a verisimilar image of as
much of the past as the evidence makes recoverable.
The latter task is the easier one. For the historian
history becomes only that part of the human past
which can be meaningfully reconstructed from the
available records and from inferences regarding their
setting.

Historical Method and Historiography Defined

The process of critically examining and analyzing
the records and survivals of the past is here called
historical method. The imaginative reconstruction of
the past from the data derived by that process is called
historiography (the writing of history). By means of
historical method and *historiography* (both of which
are frequently grouped together simply as *historical*

method)[1] the historian endeavors to reconstruct as much of the past of mankind as he can. Even in this limited effort, however, the historian is handicapped. He rarely can tell the story even of a part of the past "as it actually occurred," although the great German historian Leopold von Ranke enjoined him to do so, because in addition to the probable incompleteness of the records, he is faced with the inadequacy of the human imagination and of human speech for such an "actual" re-creation. But he can endeavor, to use a geometrician's phrase, to approach the actual past "as a limit." For the past conceived of as something that "actually occurred" places obvious limits upon the kinds of record and of imagination that he may use. He must be sure that his records really come from the past and are in fact what they seem to be and that his imagination is directed toward *re-creation* and not creation. These limits distinguish history from fiction, poetry, drama, and fantasy.

Imagination in Historiography

The historian is not permitted to imagine things that could not reasonably have happened. For certain purposes that we shall later examine he may imagine

---

[1] Some confusion arises from the use of the term *historical method* by practitioners in other disciplines (economics and theology especially) to mean the application of historical data and illustrations to their problems. It will simplify our discussion to restrict the term to the method by which historical testimony is analyzed for authentic and credible data. Courses by historians in "historical method," however, generally include not only instruction in such analysis but also the synthesizing of such data into reliable historical expositions and narratives.

things that might have happened. But he is frequently required to imagine things that must have happened. For the exercise of the imagination in history it is impossible to lay down rules except very general ones. It is a platitude that the historian who knows contemporary life best will understand past life best. Since the human mentality has not changed noticeably in historic times, present generations can understand past generations in terms of their own experience. Those historians can make the best analogies and contrasts who have the greatest awareness of possible analogies and contrasts — that is, the widest range of experience, imagination, wisdom, and knowledge. Unfortunately, no platitude tells how to acquire a wide range of those desirable qualities and knowledge or how to transfer them to an understanding of the past. For they are not accumulated alone by precept or example, industry and prayer, though all of these may help. And so historiography,[2] the *synthesizing* of historical data into narrative or expositions by writing history books and articles or delivering history lectures, is not easily made the subject of rules and regulations. Some room must be left for native talent and inspiration, and perhaps that is a good thing. But since precepts and examples may help, an effort will be made (see especially Chapters VII–XI) to set forth a few of them.

---

[2] Confusion arises here too from the fact that *historiography* is sometimes used to mean the critical examination of history books already written, as, for example, in college courses on "historiography."

History of Historical Method

Historical method, however, not only can be made the subject of rules and regulations; for over two thousand years it has been. Thucydides, who in the fifth century B.C. wrote his famous history of the Peloponnesian War, conscientiously told his readers how he gathered his materials and what tests he used to separate truth from fiction. Even when he invented speeches to put into the mouths of contemporaries, he tried to make them as like the originals as his sources of knowledge permitted. He hoped to conform both to the spirit of the speaker and the letter of the speech; but since stenographic reports were not available, he had sometimes to supply the speaker's words, "expressed as I thought he would be likely to express them." [3]

Since Thucydides' day, many historians have written, briefly or at length, upon historical method. Outstanding examples are Lucian, Ibn Khaldun, Bodin, Mably, Voltaire, and Ranke, though sometimes their studies have dealt with the scope rather than the techniques of history. With Ernst Bernheim's *Lehrbuch der historischen Methode und der Geschichtsphilosophie* (1st ed., Leipzig, 1889), the modern and more academic discussion of the subject may be said to have begun. Since Bernheim's exposition a number of other textbooks have been published. Although none of them surpass his masterpiece, peculiar merits intended for particular kinds of readers are found in

[3] *Thucydides Translated into English* by Benjamin Jowett, I (Oxford, 1900), 16 (Bk. I, 22).

some. Notable examples are the Langlois and Seignobos volume for Frenchmen; the Johnson and the
Nevins volumes for Americans; the Harsin and the
Kent booklets for younger students; and the Wolf,
the Hockett, and the Bloch and Renouvin books for
students of specialized fields of history.

In all of these works and literally dozens of others
like them there is a striking degree of unanimity regarding the methods of *historical analysis*. For our
purposes these methods will be considered under four
headings: (1) the selection of a subject for investigation; (2) the collection of probable sources of information on that subject; (3) the examination of
those sources for genuineness (either in whole or in
part); and (4) the extraction of credible particulars
from the sources (or parts of sources) proved genuine. The synthesis of the particulars thus derived is
historiography, about which there is less unanimity
among the textbooks. For purposes of clarity we shall
have to treat analysis and synthesis as if they were
discrete processes, but we shall see that at various
stages they cannot be entirely separated.

Sources

The historian's problems in choosing a subject and
collecting information upon it (the latter sometimes
dignified by the Greek name of *heuristics*) will be discussed in Chapter IV. Historical heuristics do not differ essentially from any other bibliographical exercise
in so far as printed books are concerned. The historian,
however, has to use many materials that are not in
books. Where these are archeological, epigraphical,

or numismatical materials, he has to depend largely on museums. Where they are official records, he may have to search for them in archives, courthouses, governmental libraries, etc. Where they are private papers not available in official collections, he may have to hunt among the papers of business houses, the muniment rooms of ancient castles, the prized possessions of autograph collectors, the records of parish churches, etc. Having some subject in mind, with more or less definite delimitation of the persons, areas, times, and functions (i.e., the economic, political, intellectual, diplomatic, or other occupational aspects) involved, he looks for materials that may have some bearing upon those persons in that area at that time functioning in that fashion. These materials are his *sources*. The more precise his delimitations of persons, area, time, and function, the more relevant his sources are likely to be (see below, pp. 196–8).

The Distinction between Primary and Original Sources

Written and oral sources are divided into two kinds: primary and secondary. A *primary source* is the testimony of an eyewitness, or of a witness by any other of the senses, or of a mechanical device like the dictaphone — that is, of one who or that which was present at the events of which he or it tells (hereafter called simply *eyewitness*). A *secondary source* is the testimony of anyone who is not an eyewitness — that is, of one who was not present at the events of which he tells. A primary source must thus have been produced by a contemporary of the events it narrates. It does not, however, need to be original in the legal sense of the word original [4] — that is, the very document (usually the first written draft) whose contents are the subject of discussion — for quite often a later copy or a printed edition will do just as well; and in the case of the Greek and Roman classics seldom are any but later copies available.

"Original" is a word of so many different meanings that it would have been better to avoid it in precise historical discourse. It can be, and frequently is, used to denote five different conditions of a document, all of which are important to the historian. A document may be called "original" (1) because it contains fresh and creative ideas, (2) because it is not translated from the language in which it was first written, (3) because it is in its earliest, unpolished stage, (4) because its text is the approved text, unmodified and untampered with, and (5) because it is the earliest available source of the information it provides. These five meanings of the word may overlap, but they are not synonymous.

Unfortunately, the phrase "original sources" has become common among historians, and it is desirable to define its usage accurately. It is best used by the historian in only two senses — (1) to describe a source, unpolished, uncopied, untranslated, as it issued from the hands of the authors (e.g., the *original* draft of the Magna Carta) or (2) a source that gives the earliest available information (i.e., the origin) regarding the question under investigation because earlier sources

---

[4] Cf. John H. Wigmore, *Student's Textbook of the Law of Evidence* (Chicago, 1935), pp. 225–6.

have been lost (in the sense that Livy is an "original source" for some of our knowledge of the kings of Rome). In using the phrase historians are frequently guilty of looseness. An effort will be made to use it here only in the two senses just defined.

Primary sources need not be original in either of these two ways. They need be "original" only in the sense of *underived or first-hand as to their testimony*. This point ought to be emphasized in order to avoid confusion between original sources and primary sources. The confusion arises from a particularly careless use of the word *original*. It is often used by historians as a synonym for *manuscript* or *archival*. Yet a moment's reflexion will suffice to indicate that a manuscript source is no more likely to be primary than a printed source, and that it may be a copy rather than the "original." Even where it is a primary source, it may deal with a subject upon which earlier information is already available. Hence a manuscript source is not necessarily "original" in either of the two relevant senses of that word. It should be remembered that the historian when analyzing sources is interested chiefly in *particulars* and that he asks of each particular whether it is based on first-hand or second-hand testimony. Hence it makes small difference to him whether a document is "original" in the sense of "as written by its actual author" or a copy, except in so far as such originality may aid him to determine its author and therefore whether it is primary or, if secondary, from what more independent testimony it is derived. Students of history readily depend upon specialists in editorial skills and archival techniques to publish collections of manuscripts and are willing to use them in printed form.

Primary Particulars Rather than Whole Primary Sources Sought

As has just been indicated, the historian is less concerned with a source as a whole than with the particular data within that source. It is easy to conceive of a source essentially primary that will contain secondary (and therefore less usable) data. The general who writes a communiqué thereby provides a source that may be for the most part primary but for many details secondary, because he must necessarily depend upon his subordinates for information regarding much that he reports. The newspaper correspondent may, like Aeneas, tell about things "all of which he saw and part of which he was" and yet may also have to depend upon "an official spokesman" or "a source usually considered reliable" for some of his information. The careful historian will not use all the statements of such military communiqués or newspaper dispatches with equal confidence. On the other hand, should he find, as he frequently does, that a book that is essentially secondary (like a biography or even a work of fiction) contains, for example, personal letters or touches of directly observed local color, he may well use them as first-hand evidence if they are genuine and relevant.

Sources, in other words, whether primary or secondary, are important to the historian because they contain primary particulars (or at least suggest leads to primary particulars). The particulars they furnish are trustworthy not because of the book or article or report they are in, but because of the reliability of the narrator as a witness of those particulars. This point will be elaborated later (see pp. 139–44).

The Document

The word *document* (from *docere,* to teach) has also been used by historians in several senses. On the one hand, it is sometimes used to mean a written source of historical information as contrasted with oral testimony or with artifacts, pictorial survivals, and archeological remains. On the other, it is sometimes reserved for only official and state papers such as treaties, laws, grants, deeds, etc. Still another sense is contained in the word *documentation,* which, as used by the historian among others, signifies any process of proof based upon any kind of source whether written, oral, pictorial, or archeological. For the sake of clarity, it seems best to employ the word *document* in the last, the most comprehensive meaning, which is etymologically correct, using *written document* and *official document* to designate the less comprehensive categories. Thus *document* becomes synonymous with *source,* whether written or not, official or not, primary or not.

The "Human" and the "Personal" Document

The *human document* has been defined as "an account of individual experience which reveals the individual's actions as a human agent and as a participant in social life." [5] The personal document has been defined as "any self-revealing record that intentionally or unintentionally yields information regarding the structure, dynamics and functioning of the author's mental life." [6] The first definition is by a sociologist and emphasizes "experience . . . in social life" as an element of the *human document*. The second definition is by a psychologist and emphasizes "the author's mental life" as an element of the *personal document*. Yet the words *human document* and *personal document* have been used interchangeably.[7] The two kinds of documents seem to have one essential characteristic in common; a human, personal reaction to the events with which they deal. To both sociologist and psychologist it is the

[5] Herbert Blumer, *An Appraisal of Thomas and Znaniecki's 'The Polish Peasant in Europe and America'* ("Critiques of Research in the Social Sciences," Vol. I; New York, 1939), p. 29.

[6] Gordon W. Allport, *The Use of Personal Documents in Psychological Science* (New York, Social Science Research Council, 1941), p. xii.

[7] Robert Redfield, "Foreword" to Blumer, p. viii. Cf. Allport, pp. xii–xiv. Allport says that for the psychologist methods of evaluation differ for first-person and third-person documents. They revolve around "sources of material, observer reliability, and techniques of presentation." For the historian, who as nearly as possible limits his elementary data to primary particulars, these are likely to be quantitative rather than qualitative differences. That is to say, a participant in a battle will probably have more numerous first-hand data to give than a newspaper correspondent (who, incidentally, may be less mistaken than the participant). Still, a first-person account by a participant is valuable, as evidence, only for the particulars which that participant gives on first-hand testimony or for leads to first-hand testimony; and a third-person account of the same battle by a newspaper correspondent is valuable, as evidence, only for the same kind of data. Allport agrees that "the first-person and third-person documents . . . both deal with the single case and on this question will stand or fall together." See also Allport, pp. 19–20.

degree of subjectivity in these documents that distinguishes them from other documents. The best examples [8] seem to be documents written in the first person — like autobiographies and letters — or documents written in the third person but describing human reactions and attitudes — like newspaper accounts, court records, and records of social agencies.

To the historian the difference between first-person and third-person documents is not of major significance. That is true for at least three reasons. (1) Often an apparently third-person document is in fact first-person (as, for example, the *Mémoires* of Lafayette or *The Education of Henry Adams*). (2) Genuinely third-person documents in so far as they are "historicable" [9] must ultimately rest on first-hand observation (whether by the author or by someone consulted by the author).[10] (3) Every document, no matter how thoroughly the author strove to be impartial and detached, must exhibit to a greater or lesser extent the author's philosophies and emphases, likes and dislikes, and hence betrays the author's inner personality.[11] Edward Gibbon's *Decline and Fall of the Roman Empire*, Johann Gustav Droysen's *Geschichte Alexanders des Grossen* or Hippolyte Taine's *French Revolution*

---

[8] Allport, p. xiii; Blumer, p. 29.

[9] I have had to invent this word to designate "capable of critical examination by the historian." Please note that it is not a synonym for *true, reliable,* or *probable,* but means only *subject to inquiry as to credibility.*

[10] See note 7 above.

[11] Cf. Havelock Ellis, *Dance of Life* (Boston, 1923), pp. 8–12, where the different interpretations of Napoleon by H. G. Wells and Élie Faure are attributed to the difference between Wells and Faure.

may be regarded as secondary, third-person accounts of remote history, or they may be (and indeed have been) [12] regarded as autobiographical writings of Gibbon, Droysen, and Taine. Scholarly reviews of scholarly books ought to be among the least likely places to hunt for personal reactions (except, as sometimes happens with the best reviews, the reviewer deliberately sets out to present his own point of view); and yet how often private philosophies, attitudes, likes, and dislikes are unintentionally betrayed by the most sober reviewers! Whether a document is to be examined for what it reveals about its subject or for what it reveals about its author — whether, in other words, it is a third-person or a first-person document — thus depends upon the examiner's rather than the author's intention.

For the same reason the term *personal document* is to the historian synonymous with the term *human document*. These terms were invented by social scientists. The historian is not likely to employ them. To him they appear tautalogous. All documents are both human and personal, since they are the work of human beings and shed light upon their authors as well

---

[12] Cf. J. W. Swain, "Edward Gibbon and the Decline of Rome," *South Atlantic Quarterly*, XXXIX (1940), 77–93; John R. Knipfing, "German Historians and Macedonian Imperialism," *American Historical Review*, XXXI (1921), 659–61; Louis Gottschalk, "French Revolution: Conspiracy or Circumstance" in *Persecution and Liberty, Essays in Honor of George Lincoln Burr* (New York, 1931), pp. 445–52. Cf. J. H. Randall and George Haines, "Controlling Assumptions in the Practice of American Historians," Merle Curti *et al.*, pp. 17–52, and H. K. Beale, "What Historians Have Said about the Causes of the Civil War," ibid., pp. 55–92.

as upon the subjects the authors were trying to ex-
pound. Sometimes, indeed, they betray the author's
personality, private thoughts, and social life more re-
vealingly than they describe the things he had under
observation. Here, too, a document's significance may
have a greater relationship to the intention of the historian than to that of the author. Sometimes the historian may learn more about the author than the author intended that he should.[13]

---

[13] Cf. Allport, pp. 111–12, where the "unintentional personal
document" is discussed.

CHAPTER IV

CHOOSING A SUBJECT AND FINDING INFORMATION UPON IT

The Choice of a Subject

PROFESSORS of history frequently keep lists of subjects that they would like to have students investigate; publishers and editors sometimes have titles of prospective books and articles in mind for their authors. The inexperienced writer would be well advised, however, to be guided not by some teacher's, publisher's, or editor's perference but by his own, unless he wishes to run the risk (which on the stylistic side is very great) of impeding his self-expression.

The beginner, with or without aid, can easily discover a subject that interests him and that will be worthy of investigation — at least at an introductory level. He needs only to ask himself four sets of questions:

(1) The first set of questions is geographical. They center around the interrogative: "Where?" What area of the world do I wish to investigate? The Far East? Brazil? My country? My city? My neighborhood?

(2) The second set of questions is biographical. They center around the interrogative: "Who?" What persons am I interested in? The Chinese? The Greeks? My ancestors? My neighbors? A famous individual?

(3) The third set of questions is chronological. They center around the interrogative: "When?" What pe-

riod of the past do I wish to study? From the beginnings till now? The fifth century B. C.? The Middle Ages? The 1780's? Last year?

(4) The fourth set of questions is functional or occupational. They center around the interrogative: "What?" What spheres of human interest concern me most? What kinds of human activity? Economics? Literature? Athletics? Sex? Politics?

The answers to these four sets of questions will give the inquirer some notion of the limits of his historical interests. The neophyte is likely to be overambitious, largely because his lack of experience has not yet permitted him to guess the amazing amount of testimony that may be available on the subject of his choice. More rarely, the beginner may find himself discouraged by his inability to uncover enough material to justify even a meager report. But a subject can be reduced in scope, if the material is too abundant for convenient management, by reducing (1) the geographical area, (2) the number of persons, (3) the span of time, or (4) the kinds of human activity involved. And a subject upon which it is hard to find sources of information may be expanded in any of the same four directions.

Reducing a Subject's Scope

A single example will probably suffice to clarify this process. (It is deliberately chosen from a field of history in which the reader may be assumed to have both some interest and a fair degree of personal knowledge, but the novice interested in more remote problems of history does not need to have an equal degree of

knowledge to begin with.) Suppose you answered the
the question on the area of your investigation by "The
United States," and the one on persons by "The armed
forces," and the one on time by "The Second World
War," and the one on kinds of activity by "land warfare." Your area of interest then would be the history
of the military activity of the armed forces of the
United States in the Second World War. You would
soon probably find that the materials available in your
library were so numerous that you could not possibly
write anything new or penetrating on so vast a subject
in any reasonable length of time. You might then consider reducing the geographical area of interest from
the United States to your own state, the *personae dra-
matis* from the undefined armed forces to the National Guard, the time span from the Second World
War to the year 1940–1, and the scope of activity from
land warfare to military organization. Your subject
now would be limited to the organization of the National Guard of your state in the year 1940–1. If you
needed to, you could narrow that still further — to
your city, to a single regiment, to the first half of the
year, to the financial or the logistical organization, etc.

By this third step you might get a subject so narrow
that it would perhaps have appeal only for the local
patriot or specialist, but it would be of manageable
proportions in a short period of time and would probably be one upon which you could write something
that would not be easily available in a number of other
books. For classroom purposes and for beginners in
general, that is the best kind of subject, since it throws
the writer largely on his own resources without mak-

ing exorbitant demands upon him. But it would be a mistake to induce hopeful beginners in historiography to think that good history consists only of writings upon highly specialized and local subjects. That would mean inducing them to be as unimaginative as "the fantastical scholar" described in Act III, Scene III, of John Webster's *Duchess of Malfi* who strove to find out "how many knots was in Hercules' club, of what color Achilles' beard was, or whether Hector were not troubled with the tooth-ache" and who had "studied himself half blear-ey'd to know the true symmetry of Caesar's nose by a shoeing-horn."

Expanding a Subject's Scope

To avoid that extreme it should be borne in mind that the process of reducing an ambitious subject to manageable proportions can be reversed if the subject is so trivial or specialized that testimony regarding it is inadequate. If, therefore, your interest in history began, for instance, with curiosity about the citation your father won in the Second World War, and you found that your library contained very little about that citation, you might expand your subject to include your father's regiment and perhaps not stop with its rôle merely in the Second World War but trace its history from the beginnings to the present. Thus you might produce an authoritative regimental history, or going even farther, you might inquire into the part played by military decorations in the history of human warfare. A work of that scope, if well done, would interest not only patriots and historians, but soldiers, psychologists, sociologists, dramatists, and other kinds of specialists. Intensive specialized historical research upon small incidents and among particularized documents would be necessary, however, before a report on the broader subject could be written, unless it were to be copied or paraphrased from other writers.

Some wit has differentiated historical research from plagiarism by defining research as copying from more than one book, but for our purposes the essential difference lies in looking for some new or unused sources of information upon a subject or some new interpretation of it, or both. That quest is better achieved for practice purposes in a short time by modestly contracting rather than pretentiously expanding the scope of one's investigation. But if once one learns to quarry a humble block of stone one can hope someday to build a great cathedral.

Limitations upon the Choice of Subject

The desire of conscientious historians to avoid too great dependence on other writers — in other words, to make an original contribution to the study of history — suggests other questions that should be answered in choosing a subject. It would be an obvious error to select a subject upon which the testimony could be expected to be in a language that the investigator did not know and did not expect to learn; and that would hold true not merely if the language in question were of a foreign country but also if it were the technical terminology (medicine, theology, statistics, etc.) of a branch of knowledge that the writer did not intend or found it impossible to master. Similarly, if the testimony were available only in an area that would be difficult of access, or could be presumed to have disappeared, or might be costly to acquire, or belonged to private individuals who were jealous of it, or was among the restricted documents in governmental archives, frustration might be anticipated and avoided.

Sometimes beginners, moved by a commendable desire to write on some problem of lasting significance, choose subjects that are high-sounding but intangible, debatable, and answerable, if at all, only by mature judgment rather than by the scrupulous weighing of historical testimony. Such problems as "influence," "race," "class," "greatness," "cause," "motives," and "culture" are legitimate for historians to study (and some of them will be discussed below) but they and the technical difficulties they involve are better understood after the ability to distinguish between credible and incredible testimony has been learned, and they do not make good lessons for the acquisition of that ability.

The Complexity of Comparative Studies

The technical difficulties are perhaps even greater when a subject in comparative history is chosen, because even the simplest problem of comparison might involve a triple knowledge. If, for the sake of simple illustration, one wished to decide whether Napoleon Bonaparte weighed more or less than Wellington, one would first have to find out how heavy Bonaparte was, then how heavy Wellington was (each measurement requiring perhaps extensive research in different kinds of sources), and then one might have to spend even more time trying to reduce French units of weight and English units of weight of that day to some norm to which the twentieth century is accustomed. The history of prices is strewn with comparative problems of that kind. More intangible comparative studies would probably be correspondingly more complex. No matter how intriguing, such problems should be avoided by the beginning investigator or broken down into their component parts with the intention of starting modestly with one alone of the three components.

Aids in the Choice of Subject

A conscientious novice, too, might wish to discover, before he becomes engaged too deeply, whether the field of investigation in which his subject lies has been so thoroughly exploited that the chances of saying something new or different are quite limited. Expert advice would be helpful in such a case and is usually available in person or by mail. Sometimes books suggest historical problems that are in need of further clarification. Such a book is *Historical Scholarship in America, Its Needs and Opportunities* (New York, 1932) edited by Arthur M. Schlesinger, Sr. (unfortunately now sadly out of date). The bibliographies in each of the volumes summing up scholarship in the respective eras of history in the series "Clio, Introduction aux Études Historiques" (Presses Universitaires), and in the series "Rise of Modern Europe" (ed. W. L. Langer, Harper) contain suggestions for new investigations, as often is true also of the bibliographies of monographic studies. Sometimes reviews of new books and bibliographical articles in historical periodicals are likely to indicate problems that might repay further investigation in the field under discussion.

Adaptation of Title to Exposition

Later (see p. 142) we shall see why you should think of your subject in the initial stages of investigation not as a topic but as a question. Thus, continuing, for the sake of example, the subject suggested above, you might ask: "How was the National Guard of the State of New York financed in the year 1940–1?" In the course of your investigation, you might find enough data to enable you to answer that question without special emphasis upon private, local, state, federal, or other sources, and hence you might give the resulting article or book a topical title such as "The Financing of the National Guard of the State of New York in 1940–1." But suppose you ran into unexpected ramifications. Suppose the account books of one regiment showed that its expenses had been paid by a local patron and you became so absorbed that you gave nearly all your space to that one regiment and its patron, treating the other regiments and their sources of income only casually. You would then be ill-advised to call your exposition "The Financing of the National Guard of the State of New York in 1940–1." It would disarm critics, who might otherwise (justly) charge you with promising more than you delivered and (unjustly) overlook the really new information you had to present, if you renamed your presentation so as to give it a more strictly descriptive title. "The 'X' Regiment of the New York National Guard and Its Patron (1940–1)" would be a title that would lead to no greater expectations than you could now fulfill, and you would avoid a possible reviewer's displeasure because he found less than he was led to expect in your work. Even when, for literary or commercial effect, a "catchy" title is desired, too great departure from the contents of one's actual story should be carefully avoided; otherwise the possible commercial attractiveness is likely to be counterbalanced by the disappointment of the reviewers. "Patron of the Regiment" or "Mr. Smith and the 'X' Regiment" might be attractive enough as a title without misleading the reader regarding the subject matter it covered.

How to Find Sources

Having chosen a question to study, the beginner is faced with the problem of getting information that might enable him to answer that question. The historian's usual research laboratory is the library, and his most useful tool there is the library catalogue. Books have been written especially to enable the library user to exploit it to the utmost. Such a book is the *Guide to the Use of Libraries* by Margaret Hutchins, A. A. Johnson, and M. S. Williams (5th ed.; New York, 1936). An important thing to remember about a library catalogue, where it is true, is that it contains entries for subjects and book titles as well as for authors. Hence, if one has a number of key words in mind that are implied in one's subject, one might find relevant books and articles catalogued under each of these key words. Since every historical subject contains some indication of the persons, places, periods of time, and kinds of human occupation involved, four sets of headings can easily be drawn up under which to consult a catalogue for relevant book titles as well as authors. Thus, for the history of the military activity of the armed forces of the United States in the Second World War, headings like "Eisenhower" and "Mac-Arthur"; "Europe," "New Caledonia," and "Greenland"; the years 1941 to 1945; and "army," "infantry," and "land forces" are likely to be relevant (along with so many others, in this case, as to suggest that the subject might well be further limited so as to make it manageable).

Reference books also may be consulted under these keywords or headings. Such books are conveniently listed in I. G. Mudge, *Guide to Reference Books* (6th ed. and supplements; Chicago, 1936–41). Encyclopedias, dictionaries of biography, the indexes of historical monographs, atlases, etc., may all be better exploited if the user has in mind a set of places and persons to look up. Historical bibliographies, on the other hand, are most likely to be arranged according to periods of history (generally within specified areas). There are many historical bibliographies — some on periods of history, some on the history of countries, some on prominent persons, some on quite restricted subjects. The more important ones are listed in E. M. Coulter and Melanie Gerstenfeld, *Historical Bibliographies: a Systematic and Annotated Guide* (Berkeley, Cal., 1935).

By a careful use of a good library catalogue and of books like that of Hutchins, Johnson, and Williams on libraries, Mudge on reference books, and Coulter and Gerstenfeld on bibliographies, one may relatively easily begin a list of books and article titles dealing with nearly any subject. Encyclopedias, historical dictionaries, and bibliographies will provide further titles. The books and articles that are thus discovered will, in their turn, provide the names of other books and articles in their footnotes and bibliographies. The library catalogues, the bibliographies, and the footnotes of the more scholarly monographs at least may also give some indication of the relevant manuscript collections and archives that might be exploited. For more up-to-date titles, reviews and bibliographical data in the recent numbers of learned periodicals and the indexes to recent and current periodical literature (of which there are several) have to be consulted.

A Working Bibliography

All of this heuristical apparatus suggests the advisability of carrying around in one's head a short bibliography of relatively indispensable books for serious historical research. In general, it suffices for the beginner to memorize the titles of:

1. a bibliography of bibliographies (preferably the one that is most useful in his field of special interest);

2. a large printed library catalogue;

3. a good encyclopedia in his field;

4. a good dictionary of biography;

5. a good historical dictionary;

6. a good dictionary in the departmental field (economics, theology, sociology, literature, etc.) in which his historical interests lie;

7. a good dictionary on historical principles (i.e.,

one giving the history of words and the dates of new usage);

8. the historical bibliography to which he will make the most frequent reference;

9. the large general history (usually a symposium) to which he will make the most frequent reference;

10. the leading historical periodical in his field;

11. the current national bibliography (i.e., the formal announcement by publishers or some governmental agency of current publications) to which he will make the most frequent reference;

12. the periodical index to which he will make the most frequent reference;

13. the leading collection of published documents in his field.

An inexperienced historian would be well advised to prepare such a list in writing. In the belief that it will be more useful to the beginner to make his own list, no sample bibliography will be provided here, but there are literally thousands of titles from which a possible choice may be made. The books on such a list will lead the compiler to other titles, and from their combined bibliographical suggestions, he can build a complete and up-to-date bibliography of articles and monographs (as well as more general literature) on any subject.

Note-taking

The most dreary part of the historian's work is the taking of notes, and it is at least as desirable to learn when not to take notes or to take only brief ones as it is to learn when to take full ones. Three general observations may be helpful.

(1) The temptation to takes notes on material that is interesting often consumes time that might better be used for notes that are relevant, whether interesting or not. Hence strict standards of relevance should be constantly borne in mind. This is not an easy thing to do and will require further discussion (see pp. 195–201).

(2) Full notes should not be taken on data that are familiar, unauthoritative (except for the purpose of rebuttal), or easily remembered. But a word of caution is desirable here. Beginners are highly likely to overestimate their ability to remember and therefore may spend many subsequent hours looking for vaguely recollected items upon which precision is now wanted.

(3) Wherever the likelihood exists that the exact words of a source may be quoted in the final composition, a full note of the quotable material is called for. The exact words of a passage are most likely to be quoted when they are especially picturesque, authoritative, unfamiliar, hard to remember, subject to dispute, or contradictory of the usually accepted story.

The Quoted Note

In general a full note should be a meticulous one. The language of the source should be carefully copied, since less hurried and more pat translations can be made at the time of actual composition. The source's spelling, orthography, and punctuation should be studiously retained. The hard-working little word *sic* (meaning *thus*, and which in this usage is always underlined and placed inside brackets) should be readily employed to denote errors that have occurred in the source; otherwise upon future reference to the note one might be unable to tell whether a then obvious error was the source's or the note-maker's. The ellipsis (. . .) should be used to indicate that words occurring in the source have been deliberately omitted by the note-taker. Underlinings generally indicate that the words underlined were in italics in the source. Where the ellipsis is in the source or the underlining is that of the note-maker and not of the source, this should be indicated within brackets immediately after the ellipsis or underlining. In general, all words inserted within a quotation by the note-taker should be placed inside brackets. If a note runs over more than one page of the source, it is desirable to indicate by an oblique line (/) where the break in pagination occurs, since the parts that may be quoted in the future composition may come from either one rather than from both pages quoted.

Photographic Reproduction

If the desired material is lengthy, the note-taker might consider using a photographic process such as the photostat or the microfilm for reproducing the written or printed page. Many academic and metropolitan libraries provide such facilities at relatively low cost; and they will become very common, despite the inevitable professional "lag" in their adoption by historians used to books and manuscripts. It has long been possible to place a good-sized article (or chapter) on a single micro-reproduction card; and already a machine known as the Microfilm Rapid Selector has been constructed and put in use in the United States Department of Agriculture. This machine can automatically sort and select wanted materials from reels of microfilm at the rate of more than 10,000 reproductions per minute if the classification system is properly organized; and another machine known as the Ultrafax can transmit microfilmed materials through space at the speed of light and at the rate of about 1,000,000 words per minute, as well as charts, maps, illustrations, and diagrams. Both machines also provide for ready reproduction of permanent and readable photographs of the selected materials. "Thus the bibliographic item available anywhere can be almost instantaneously available everywhere and the problem of supply for the scholar without a large research library may be solved." [1]

The historians of earlier periods of history will still be limited by the poverty of materials. A machine that transmits 1,000,000 words a minute is not much use to an investigator of a subject upon which there are fewer words than a million available anywhere. But for more recent fields of history — and especially twentieth-century history — the problem of rapid assorting and transmission is becoming acute. Records of the Second World War, for example, were transported from the European theater of operations to Washington literally by the freight carload and now are being compiled

---

[1] "Bibliographical Services in the Social Sciences: a Report to the Carnegie Corporation by the Graduate Library School and the Division of the Social Sciences of the University of Chicago, September, 1949" (mimeographed), p. 26.

into official histories in numerous huge tomes by teams of historians. The future writer of monographs from this material will have to devise categories and sampling techniques that may now seem fantastic to the conventional historians.[2]

The Reminder Note

Usually a note is taken as a mere reminder of material that is not going to be quoted. Hence it is sufficient merely to indicate its source without copying its exact language. The note may be very simple if the source is the note-taker's own property or belongs to a library to which he has ready access, for in that case it need be only a sort of index-card. E.g.:

Collingwood, *Idea of History*, 190–4

Critique of Croce's 1893 essay on history

Since the book is itself easily available, it will probably mean an ultimate saving of time and exasperation to

[2] Cf. W. S. Holt, "An Evaluation of the Report on Theory and Practice in Historical Study," *Pacific Historical Review*, XVIII (1949), 239–43.

return to the book itself if the occasion should arise rather than to make a full analysis at the time of note-taking. For parallel reasons, when a book is not available, because, let's say, it is out of print and is borrowed from a distant library, a fuller analysis of relevant material is desirable. If it seems fairly clear both that the desired information is relevant and that it may be easy to remember, a careful paraphrase in the note-taker's words may suffice. Yet one is also well-advised to consider verbatim quotations (with ellipses, if desirable) or photographic reproduction, for one never knows but that exact quotation may appear preferable when composition is under way and the book is no longer easily available.

Labor Saving Devices and Cross References

A conscientious note-taker soon learns little effort-saving devices. Time and mental exertion can frequently be saved by indicating, in cases where it may not be obvious, why the note was taken, lest a point that seemed self-evident at first encounter should at some future time defy detection. In that way one can circumvent the sense of frustration that experienced note-takers sometimes encounter when they find among their notes painstaking quotations that now cause only wonder as to why the pains were once considered worth taking. The writing of notes to oneself suggesting queries, insertions, hypotheses, pat sentences, cross references, and the brilliant ideas that come in the middle of the night (and probably appear drab in the morning) might also be cultivated to advantage — if desirable, on separate note slips to be appropriately filed with the reference notes. Documents should also be "analyzed" — that is, sifted for references to various events and persons. A single note, for example, to a letter that contains a passing reference to earlier events or to several personalities might be filed only under the name of the writer of the letter, and the references to the earlier events or other personalities might be lost sight of unless they were separately noted or "cross referenced." In general, cross references are best made as soon as the possibility of their usefulness becomes apparent; otherwise the danger is great that they will be forgotten.

Bibliographical Notes

Notes giving titles of books and articles that are or may be relevant to one's investigation should be of two kinds — (1) those on titles to be used and (2) those on titles that have been used. The first, derived from various bibliographical aids, need contain only enough information to enable the investigator to identify the item; taking a fuller note might mean a waste of time, since the title might prove upon examination to be valueless. When, from actual examination of the book or article, one has discovered that the work is going to be useful, a full bibliographical note becomes desirable. Such a note should contain all the data that may be required for careful footnotes and bibliographies. Schools, periodicals, and publishers differ regarding what should go into a bibliographical item and in what order. It is wise therefore to find out what style your prospective teacher or editor prefers. Frequently a "style-sheet" or a "manual of style" is made available by schools, editors, and publishers and should be consulted. The Alfred A. Knopf, Inc. style-sheet is given below in the Appendix.

Once a note has been taken with the exact bibliographical data of an item that is actually going to be used by the investigator, he need not in his future notes from that item give the full bibliographical data again. An abbreviated title will be sufficient; e.g., "Collingwood, *Idea of History*" will suffice for "R. G. Collingwood, *The Idea of History* (Oxford: Clarendon Press, 1946)," since the fuller reference will be available in the investigator's file of "Titles Actually Consulted." When only one title by an author is used, some editors permit citations following the first one to refer to that item simply by the author's name, but in taking notes, "Collingwood" alone will not suffice, because even though you may not be aware of it at the time of note-taking, at some future time you may use another book by Collingwood and thus create a needless confusion between the two. The full bibliographical note should also contain the library call number in order to obviate the necessity of looking up the library catalogue again. Unlike context notes (see below, p. 81), bibliographical notes should be on 3″ x 5″ cards, since cards of that size are very easily handled and no single bibliographical item is likely to run over more than one such card. Filed alphabetically (by names of authors, since few research projects reach the proportions where subject titles become necessary) in a 3″ x 5″ filing box, these cards are easily moved from one compartment ("Titles to Be Consulted") to the other ("Books Actually Consulted"), fuller bibliographical data having been supplied in the interval.

Material for Notes

The 3" x 5" card is generally too small, too thick and too expensive for an efficient system of context notes. What is needed is a good paper slip that will not take up much room, will stand rough handling, and is of a size that is easily procurable, no matter to what flea-bitten library in no matter what provincial hamlet your research may take you. At the same time it should be of a size for which there exists a standard commercial filing box. A good quality of ordinary typewriter paper is just about right if it is folded in half. Its dimensions would then be approximately 8½" x 5½", which should be sufficient for the usual note, especially if both sides are used. Certainly all four sides of the folded sheet would suffice for even the most extensive notes. Hence, after being folded, the 8½" x 11" should not be torn or cut in half until it is clear that a single 8½" x 5½" slip will suffice. Otherwise the use of metal clips or staples may become necessary, and such metal devices are great inconveniences in a note-system. They tear, stain and rot paper, and, what is worse, catch on to neighboring notes, which then become difficult to find. Filing cards with tabs upon which headings may be written are also necessary to a good system of notes.

An investigator going to work in libraries with whose rules he is not familiar had also better provide himself with a good indelible pencil, because many libraries

quite properly do not allow the use of ink in their
rare book and manuscript rooms. The ordinary graph-
ite pencil is bad for note-taking; in the course of time
it rubs and smudges, becomes illegible itself, and
makes adjacent notes illegible too.

Arranging Notes

As already explained, bibliographical notes should
be filed in two sections: "Titles to Be Consulted" and
"Titles Actually Consulted." Under each of these sections, arrangement by the alphabetical order of the
authors' names is recommended for most purposes. In
context notes the chronological arrangement is usually
the best one in the early stages of investigation and
will probably prove the best one at all stages, if the
final composition is to be a narrative. Chronological
order also simplifies the problem of cross reference
when the same note may be pertinent to more than
one place in the story, since the note may be filed
under the earliest relevant date and cross referenced to
that date. Even if the dates of one's subject change in
the course of investigation, it will be relatively easy to
find the note again so long as it remains in its approximate chronological order.

By a topical arrangement cross-reference problems
become more difficult, especially as topics change in
the course of investigation. Nevertheless, a topical arrangement sometimes appears preferable, and especially if the final composition is to be argumentative or
expository. Topical arrangement may be by persons
(individuals, groups, communities, societies, etc.), by
areas, by kinds of activity, or by some combination of

these. Topics, too, may have a roughly chronological relation to each other. This would be especially true where the development of a society or an area is being described for a certain fixed period. Within the separate topics a chronological order is also usually discernible. After all, that's the way history happens.

An Illustration of Historical Organization

An illustration may make clearer in what ways topical arrangement may be preferable to the strictly chronological. Suppose the subject under discussion were the education of Louis XVI. It could be described by a chronological consideration of factors in the life of Louis XVI that might be regarded as having contributed to his education. That is the way *The Education of Henry Adams* was written. But suppose in the course of the investigation the investigator decided to limit attention to "What did Louis XVI read?" A chronological listing of Louis' reading would prove to be impossible, because the records would not always suggest *when*, even if they indicated *what* he had read. An alphabetical listing of Louis' reading also suggests itself, but since many references would be to kinds of readings rather than to specific titles or authors, such a listing might become complicated. A chronological ordering of the investigator's sources of information would also be feasible, but different sources might mention the same items or kinds of readings, and much repetition and disjointedness would result. In addition, by any of these three orderings it would be necessary to stop every time the problem presented itself to explain that some of the titles were more and some were less verifiable as actually having been read by Louis. A fourth kind of organization might therefore be preferable.

A topical arrangement would get around the difficulties of dating, repetition, and incoherence. One could divide Louis XVI's readings into categories: (1) Books, articles, etc., or authors on which the evidence was conclusive; (2) books, etc., or authors probably read but on which the evidence was debatable; (3) kinds of reading-matter indicated by the sources without specification of the separate titles (e.g., French drama); and (4) kinds of reading-matter in his library that he may or may not have read. Each category ought to be arranged in chronological order so far as possible, but its completeness would not be dependent upon the chronological arrangement.

It should not be lost to view, however, that one of the important advantages of the chronological ordering has been sacrificed here. Louis XVI's education was a dynamic process; it proceeded in a chronological fashion. If any of his readings had some kind of developmental overlapping with the others, a categorical arrangement will not bring that out. If categories could be devised (e.g., books that seem to have had some effect on Louis XVI's policies; books that were read merely for passing pleasure; etc.), both the problem of coherence and the problem of educational development could be mastered. Unfortunately in this case, as in many others, the available sources would probably not permit such an organization.

Incidentally this illustration also indicates one of the advantages of thinking of one's problem as a query rather than a subject. The relevance of particulars to an answer to a question is easier to determine than their relevance to the development of a topic. But we shall return to this subject more fully later (Chapter VII).

CHAPTER V

WHERE DOES HISTORICAL INFORMATION COME FROM?

"The Past for the Sake of the Past"

THE HISTORIAN has at least a double purpose. He is (1) a guardian of the cultural heritage and (2) a narrator of the development of mankind. In the first capacity, he is concerned with establishing as accurate, detailed, and impartial an account of past persons, events, thoughts, institutions, and things as his knowledge and critique of sources will permit. Here his motto may well be "the past for the sake of the past." Even here, however, he is faced with problems of selection (which persons, event, thought, institution, or things to study?) and of relationships among persons, events, thoughts, institutions, and things. In the second capacity, however, he has to have some theory of how mankind develops as well. Hence he finds himself deeply enmeshed in philosophy and sociology and perhaps also in considerations of a personal nature regarding selection and emphasis of material.

We shall consider later the questions of selection and emphasis and of history as a social science (see pp. 195–207 and 252–77). Here it suffices to point out that of all the social studies history is the most humanistic. Whereas an anthropologist would be interested in a potsherd chiefly because of the light it shed on a *state* of culture or an economist in a coin because of the information it gave regarding the financial *system* of the society from which it was derived, in order to fit them into some predictable trend or controlling generalization, the historian would also be interested in the potter and the coinmaker and their times for their intrinsic interest. Human beings as individuals, facts as particulars are of importance to the historian *qua* historian. Though the historian who carries his interests no farther than individuals and particulars may be merely an antiquarian, it is sometimes forgotten in historical circles that antiquarians are respectable members of the historical profession, just as geologists and paleontologists are of their professions. The historian who studies a past thing for itself alone and in isolation from other things may make a significant contribution to the knowledge not only of that thing but also of its environment, and in any case he may keep the knowledge of that thing from being lost.

Surviving Objects as Documents

To the historian (whether antiquarian or social philosopher) a piece of pottery or a coin, an ancient seal or a recent stamp may well be a "personal" document, revealing the artistic ability, the degree of literacy, perhaps even the hopes and aspirations of the man who made it or designed it. If nothing were to remain of present-day American culture a thousand years hence but a single one-cent piece, any historian of that day would nevertheless be able to make some shrewd guesses about the man who had designed the coin, and still more about the civilization in which he

lived, merely from a careful analysis of the coin itself. Even a casual glance at a Lincoln penny will suffice to prove that statement. It indicates a culture that
had some knowledge of metallurgy and agriculture; of
dies and engraving; of barbering, cloth and tailoring;
of English and Latin, and Arabic numerals; of chronology and geography; of God, liberty, and political con-
federation; of arithmetic and the decimal system. A
Jefferson nickel would confirm these indications and
would add some knowledge of architecture to the
accomplishments of the coinmaker's culture. And so
on with other American coins. Such impersonal
sources as archeological remains thus may be included
in the historian's documents. Being less fortunate than
the psychologist or sociologist in that he usually cannot place his human specimens under direct control,
he frequently has to derive his knowledge of social or
mental life from such testimony as has survived, however inadequate it may be. Frequently this testimony
takes the form of wordless things rather than words.

The analysis of historical data contained in things
that have survived from the past has become highly
specialized and will be mentioned again when we
come to consider the sciences auxiliary to history, such
as numismatics and archeology (see pp. 127–8). It
does not detract from the significance of the archeologist's contributions that curators sometimes out of an
excess of competitive zeal make claims for their possessions that cannot be substantiated. It would be interesting to weigh all the supposed pieces of the original cross of Jesus' crucifixion to see whether they do
not in fact exceed the weight that a single man could

possibly have dragged; at least two museums claim to own the original bathtub in which Marat was stabbed by Charlotte Corday; and to judge by museum claims, a number of scrupulous men seem to have scattered articles of their furniture and clothing far and wide. Insufficiently trained curators display bad judgment in such instances sometimes because of a natural readiness to accept local or family legend or to gain an unwarranted celebrity for their treasures.

Written Testimony

The historian, as distinguished from the anthropologist who is concerned with preliterate societies and the archeologist who is concerned with artifacts, deals chiefly with testimony contained in written documents. Those documents may be divided into major categories such as autobiographies, letters, newspaper accounts, stenographic reports of legislative and judicial bodies, and records of business, government, or social agencies. Each of these categories can, in its turn, be broken up into smaller groups; and there may be important differences among the lesser groups in the same categories. A diplomatic dispatch, for example, would differ in purpose, reliability, and type of recipient from a private letter; and a newspaper editorial would differ markedly from an Associated Press dispatch. In the attempt that will now be made to classify documents it has seemed desirable therefore to break the major categories into smaller groups. An effort will also be made to arrange the smaller groups in the order of their reliability. We shall assume in each case that the documents are authentic. More will be said of their reliability later (see pp. 118–71) in the discussion of the criteria of authenticity and credibility.

General Rules

Four general rules will suffice here to indicate why one group of documents may be given precedence over another. (1) As we have seen, incomplete observation and faulty memory are often responsible for the inadequacy of testimony. Because a witness's reliability is, in general, inversely proportional to the *time-lapse* between the observation of the event and the witness' recollection, the closer the time of making a document was to the event it records, the better it is likely to be for historical purposes. (2) Some documents were originally intended purely as records or aids to one's memory, some as reports to other persons, some as apologia, some as propaganda, and so on. Because documents differ in this way in *purpose*, the more serious the author's intention to make a mere record, the more dependable his document as a historical source. (3) Because the effort, on the one hand, to palliate the truth or, on the other, to decorate it with literary, rhetorical, or dramatic flourishes tends to increase as the expected audience increases, in general the fewer the number for whose eyes the document was meant (i.e., the greater its *confidential nature*), the more "naked" its contents are likely to be. (4) Because the testimony of a schooled or experienced observer and reporter (e.g., a professional soldier reporting a battle, an experienced correspondent describing an interview, a veteran policeman reporting an accident, etc.) is generally superior to that of the untrained and casual observer and reporter, the greater the *expertness* of the author in the matter he is reporting, the more reliable his report.

I. *Contemporary Records*

A *record* may be defined as a document intended to convey instructions regarding a transaction or to aid the memory of the persons immediately involved in a transaction. It is distinguished from a *report* in *time-lapse, purpose,* and the *confidential nature* of its contents. Obviously, if a record is an instruction, it is a part of the transaction (namely, the expression of a participant's wish), and the expression of the wish is frequently simultaneous with the record of it. If, however, it is an aide-memoire or memorandum, the lapse of time between the event and the recollection of the event becomes an important factor in its reliability. For that reason memoranda should perhaps more accurately be considered *reports* than *records* — especially if they are memoranda intended to jog some other person's memory.

(A) Probably the most credible type of document is the *instruction* or *command.* This may take the form of an appointment to office, a command on the field of battle, an order to a commercial house, a suggestion from a foreign office to an ambassador, a scribbled note of a trial judge to a page asking for information, a letter of a social worker giving directions to a client, a grocery order slip, etc. As to the expressed intention of the author, and even as to his state of mind in some instances, there can be little room for deceit or error in such documents. The sincerity of the expressed intention must be tested by other criteria (see pp. 155–65 below).

(B) Likewise, *stenographic and phonographic records*, whether of courts, social agencies, legislatures, radio broadcasts, committees, school faculties, or other word-using bodies, are reliable at least as to *what* was said. The *truth* and *sincerity* of what was said must be subject to other tests. It is important to bear in mind, however, that sometimes before reports purporting to be transcripts from stenographic or phonographic records are published, they have been polished and corrected. The historian, psychologist, lawyer or sociologist for whom literary style and grammatical errors may be important clues in detecting emotional stress, fatigue, confusion, or ignorance, may thus easily be misled if he accepts such a transcript fully (cf. p. 107 below).

(C) Sometimes *business and legal papers*, such as bills, journals, orders, inventories, tax records, articles of incorporation, leases, wills, etc., reveal significant data about the firms and transactions with which they deal but also about the persons involved. One can learn much, for instance, from a budget book about the mental and social life of the budgeter or from a will about the likes and dislikes of the testator. The degree of reliability to be attributed to such business and legal papers is high, not only because they frequently are prepared by experts but also because business houses generally do not care to deceive themselves and there are laws against deceiving others. Here, too, the distinction between record and report should be borne in mind. An account in one's confidential books of the cost of operating one's business may not necessarily agree with one's tax report on the same costs — and the discrepancies are not necessarily illegal.

(D) *Personal notebooks and private memoranda* kept by many individuals, particularly prominent ones, to remind them of appointments, things to do, ideas to be remembered, points to make in the next week's speech or in next year's book, literary excerpts worthy of note, and so on, are high in credibility because generally intimate and confidential, frequently close to events with which they deal, and usually innocent of effort to influence others. Glorified examples of such documents are the commonplace book of Jefferson and the notebook of Robespierre, but everyone who has kept a humble date-book, memopad, or notebook of favorite quotations has been the author (perhaps unintentionally) of a document of this nature; and if his document survives a thousand years from now, it may be one of the most prized treasures of some historian's collection.

II. *Confidential Reports*

Confidential reports differ from *records* in that they are usually written after the event, are often intended to create an impression rather than merely to aid memory, and are less intimate, even though not intended for large audiences. Hence they are less reliable, as a general rule, than *contemporary records*.

(A) Among the most reliable of reports, since they are frequently written by experts, for confidential purposes, and shortly after the events narrated, are *military and diplomatic dispatches*. These must be distinguished from communiqués intended for public consumption, where frequently the intention is to beguile rather than to inform. Rarely has a great military figure made plainer than General Dwight D. Eisenhower the difficulties that confront an officer in compiling an accurate report of his campaign experiences:

The lack of time and the demands upon the attention of all commanders and staff officers preclude the keeping of day-by-day and minute-by-minute accounts of everything that happens. Many significant actions are initiated by verbal contact, and frequently no records are kept. Battle orders, even for large formations, are often written after instructions have been issued in an exhaustive conference. Notes of the actual discussions do not exist. Moreover, later curiosity so often concerns itself with responsibility for thought and idea, rather than with events and results, that possibly even the most painstaking amanuensis could not leave any clear and unchallengeable account of all the occurrences that go to make up a campaign.[1]

(B) The *journal or diary* is said to be "the personal document par excellence" for the psychologist,[2] when spontaneous and intimate. It also ranks high as a

---

[1] From: *Crusade in Europe* by Dwight D. Eisenhower. Copyright 1948 by Doubleday & Company, Inc. P. 256. Cf. the review by E. M. Earle in the *American Historical Review*, LIV (1949), 881. (Footnotes, like this one, which break up the reference into several parts separated by periods are not recommended, but they are sometimes required by the owners of copyrights.)

[2] Allport, p. 95.

historical document if it meets those conditions. Diaries do not always meet them, however. Too often a *diary or journal*, though it is called such, contains entries under a certain date that were not made until that date had long passed, and thus is more accurately designated a *memoir*. Sometimes the diarist, far from having horror of prying eyes, may keep his diary for public consumption.[3] Or he may have kept a journal to justify himself (as did Franklin during the Franco-American peace negotiations), thus spoiling its spontaneity. Furthermore, there is always the danger that a diary when published (which is the usual form in which the historian sees it) has been "touched up" or "doctored" for political or personal reasons, and the degree of modification hidden until the original manuscript can be examined by a later historian. In general, diaries concerned with recent political crises in totalitarian countries are subject to suspicion on this score, because they may have had to omit passages or to disguise names and events in order to shield the individuals involved or to avoid libel suits.[4]

(C) *Personal letters*, too, if they are spontaneous and intimate, rank high in credibility. Since, however, they are less likely to contain the testimony of a skilled observer, frequently are intended to exert influence or to create an impression, are often not private and confidential but are intended for all the members of a family and a circle of friends, and often deal with

---

[3] E.g., William L. Shirer, *Berlin Diary; Journal of a Foreign Correspondent, 1934-1941* (New York, 1941).

[4] E.g., *Ambassador Dodd's Diary, 1933-1938*, edited by William and Martha Dodd (New York, 1941).

hearsay and remote matters, they are inferior as testimony to some other kinds of documents. In *personal letters*, too, etiquette and convention frequently require expressions of politeness and esteem that may deceive the reader not familiar with the customs of the letter-writer's region. Personal considerations may also enter more frequently to color the presentation of facts; a student writing home to his father for money or a lover writing to his beloved might not tell the unvarnished truth, even though their letters might be entirely confidential.

III. *Public Reports*

Public reports are to be distinguished from *confidential reports* chiefly by the number of persons expected (or desired) by their authors to read them. Since that number is larger, the general degree of reliability (in accordance with Rule 3 on p. 90) is less than for *confidential reports*. Compare, as a striking example, the confidential report of a general to his ministry of war with the usual kind of communiqué issued by the ministry for public consumption. Three major subdivisions of *public reports* call for special consideration.

(A) *Newspaper reports and dispatches*, intended by the reporter for the world at large, are probably the most reliable of the three because the time-lapse between event and recording is usually short. The very fact, however, which makes for that virtue — namely the obligation on newspaper reporters to write frequent, even daily, accounts — may also make for haste (and consequently carelessness of verification) or even invention. What is said of the newspaper dispatch also applies to *pamphlets, broadsheets, and chapbooks* in the era when they served some of the purposes of the newspaper, because it was not yet fully developed, or at those times in history (revolution, foreign occupation, censorship, etc.) when handier means of communication are resorted to because newspapers are restricted or suppressed.

The reliability of a newspaper dispatch may frequently be judged by the reputation of the journal in which it appears or of the press association with which it originates. Nevertheless, each dispatch should undergo, wherever possible, the tests to be outlined below (pp. 150–64) for its own credibility, for it goes without saying that a reliable dispatch may sometimes appear in a journal of generally bad reputation and an unreliable one in a journal of generally good reputation. One must also be on guard against the tendency of newspapers to give interdependent accounts of events. Until the nineteenth century, the special correspondent was relatively unknown and newspapers frankly copied from each other; now they depend more upon the same syndicated report. Hence it is seldom safe to assume, unless the reporters' names are given, that because an event is described in two newspapers, the descriptions are by two independent witnesses. Even then one cannot be sure that two (or more) reporters did not collaborate. Newspapers in recent years have made evaluation of their reports still more complicated by their practice of "policing the news" — that is, giving prominent display to news that is favorable to the owner's policies and "burying" or misleadingly headlining or rewriting news that is unfavorable.[5]

What has just been said of *newspaper dispatches* does not apply to newspapers as a whole. A newspaper consists of many different kinds of documents. Letters to the editor (which are often spurious) are to be treated as *personal letters*; advertisements as *business documents*; comics and caricatures usually as *works of fiction*;[6] editorials, book reviews, syndicated columns, and, too often, headlines[7] as *expressions of opinion*;[8] and so on.

(B) *Memoirs and autobiographies* also partake of the nature of public reports. It is, however, important to distinguish between the type of memoirs with which the historian usually deals and the type of autobiography that frequently constitutes the chief personal document of the sociologist and psychologist or the oral testimony that witnesses give in courtrooms. The living subject who narrates his autobiography under the eye or ear of the scientist or gives his testimony in reply to the questions of the lawyer, who is then able to cross-examine the narrator, who may thereupon supplement, correct, or confirm his original statements, rarely is available to the historian. Only historians who deal with relatively recent affairs may be so fortunate.

---

[5] Cf. Edgar Dale, *How to Read a Newspaper* (Chicago, 1941), p. 45.

[6] See below, pp. 112–14.

[7] See, for example, the first-page 8-column headline, "Dewey Defeats Truman" of the *Chicago Daily Tribune*, home edition, Nov. 3, 1948.

[8] See below, pp. 109–11.

Where the historian is lucky enough to have the personal testimony of a living witness, his technique of analysis greatly resembles that of the psychologist, the lawyer, or the sociologist. He may elicit information by oral questioning or interview, or from a written document supplemented by oral questioning and interview. In any case the testimony cannot be superior to the witness's ability or willingness to tell the truth, and is therefore subject to the tests of *credibility* to be described (pp. 149–65). Yet the opportunity to make a personal examination of a living memoir-writer may simplify many of the historians' problems. They then have personal corroboration of the authenticity and the meaning of the document; gaps of testimony can be pieced in; judgment of the author's competence as a first-hand witness is made easier; his inconsistencies and his contradictions of others can perhaps be harmonized or eliminated. Historians too seldom use the technique that Thucydides so ably exploited of interviewing surviving witnesses of the events they have under examination. Official historians of recent military history, however, have made frequent use of the interview.

Unfortunately the historian usually deals with autobiographies of subjects long dead or beyond personal contact. It is impossible to ask them whether certain parts of their narrative are based on their own experience or the experience of others; whether they are absolutely certain of the details they give which contradict other evidences, and why they are certain; whether their motives are to tell the unvarnished truth or to plead a special case. It is impossible to get them to clarify implications that are obscure and to supply missing links in their narratives. And yet that sort of difficulty becomes more, rather than less, acute with the more notable memoirs of history. For such memoirs were occasionally intended to appeal to a large reading public; many of them were written late in life, when memory was beginning to fade, thus making the particulars untrustworthy; [9] and very often they were apologia or polemics, thus making gravely suspect their selection, arrangement, and emphases of the particulars. When Winston Churchill, for example, published his memoirs of the Second World War, protests from American, French, Belgian, and other participants arose that he had not done full justice to "the facts." The historian or psychologist interested in the inner springs of consciousness may, however, sometimes find the idealized personality of an autobiography more meaningful than the more realistic character revealed by better sources.[10] It is also true that for the correct understanding of personal influences, cults, and legends, the idealization

---

[9] A striking illustration that memory may deceive even relatively young men came to my attention in Joseph Freeman's An American Testament; a Narrative of Rebels and Romantics (New York, 1936), p. 21. There the author refers to an incident in which I played a part. My recollection of the incident differed from Freeman's in some respects, and so I asked another witness for his version of the story. It differed from both Freeman's and mine! Such tricks of the memory perhaps help to explain why a learned judge is said to have complained that he had wasted most of his professional life trying to discover how two automobiles, each in good mechanical condition and driven by competent drivers on the correct side of the road, could meet in head-on collision.

[10] Cf. Carl Becker, "The Memoirs and the Letters of Madame Roland," American Historical Review, XXXIII (1928), 784–803.

by disciples often is a more meaningful historical fact than the actual personality (cf. below pp. 234–5).

A problem that arises to plague the historian also in connection with many other kinds of documents occurs with special frequency and brazenness in connection with memoirs. That is the problem of "ghost-writing." How much among the several versions of Napoleon's memoirs, for example, is in Napoleon's own words and how much is the creation of his several amanuenses? What part of Talleyrand's *Mémoires* were revised by the editor? In recent years, as the "ghost-writer" and the editor become more and more respectable and persistent members of the literary guild, the problem has become more acute. Perversions for journalistic purposes, suppressions to avoid bad taste, libel, or the revelation of confidential information, and elaborations for dramatic effect, thus creep in to heighten unreliability. The practice that has recently developed among outstanding American statesmen like Stimson and Stettinius of writing their memoirs in collaboration with historians of known reputation and principles may make it difficult to determine what is first-hand recollection by the alleged author and what is secondary history by the collaborator, but at least it represents a conscientious effort to achieve historical accuracy and responsibility.

(C) *Official or authorized histories* of recent activities by governmental agencies, business houses, fraternal organizations, etc., when published (i.e. not restricted as private or secret records), also share the nature of public reports. Such histories are frequently written under excellent circumstances permitting the full exploitation of official records and personages for their testimony. Yet, as a class they have marked weaknesses. In part, their weakness is derived from an understandable effort to appeal to large constituencies by making them journalistic and "timely" or "topical."

The opinion, however, is sometimes encountered in historical circles that in general the recent past, even under most favorable circumstances of investigation, is not a proper subject for the historian. That opinion is based chiefly on three arguments that must be admitted to have some validity: (a) the best sources (i.e., the most intimate and confidential ones) are seldom available until long after the periods with which they deal; (b) impartiality is exceptionally difficult when describing and judging recent events and live issues; (c) true perspective as to what is important can be the product only of the long-run. Very often history has to be rewritten not alone (as we shall see) because succeeding generations change the kind of questions they wish to ask of the past but also because new information has become available or new perspectives imperative. "Tacitus," it has been pointed out, "though endowed with extraordinary sagacity, exhibits little or no insight into the [contemporary] progress of the gigantic revolution which culminated in the establishment of Christianity throughout the Roman Empire." [11]

Yet, despite those arguments, the historian interested in a timely subject often does interview

---

[11] A. V. Dicey, *Lectures on the Relation between Law and Public Opinion in England during the Nineteenth Century* (London, 1930), p. xxiv n.

contemporaries or exploit his own experience of contemporary events,[12] and the official historian has exceptionally good facilities for doing so. There are enough classic precedents besides Tacitus for that kind of historical investigation (Thucydides, Suetonius, Bede, Einhard, Matthew Paris, Froissart, Clarendon, Voltaire, Napier, Louis Blanc, and Sybel among others) to make it possible to hope that historians of recent affairs using similar methods may even make a significant contribution to historical knowledge.

The appointment during and after the Second World War of official historians to contemporary war bodies, political and military, indicates that official authorities are less inhibited in this regard than some historians. Usually these official historians have avoided propaganda and, although not always free to say all that they wished, have avoided deliberate misrepresentation. As a general rule, however, *official histories* must be treated with caution. Not only are they liable to reveal the weaknesses inherent in investigations of subjects of current interest; they are also often largely secondary in nature, since they are based upon information only partly obtained by the author at first hand, if indeed they are not wholly dependent upon

---

[12] E.g., F. J. Turner, *The Frontier in American History* (New York, 1920); W. P. Webb, *The Great Plains* (Boston, 1931); B. E. Schmitt, *Interviewing the Authors of the War* (Chicago, 1930); E. M. House and Charles Seymour (eds.), *What Really Happened in Paris: the story of the peace conference, 1918–1919, by American delegates* (New York, 1921); Leon Trotsky, *History of the Russian Revolution*, tr. Max Eastman (3 vols.; New York, 1932); Winston Churchill, *The Second World War; The Gathering Storm* (Boston, 1948).

the analysis of others' testimony. Whenever they are in fact primary, they suffer from the shortcomings characteristic of memoirs, especially from the tendencies to suppress embarrassing, incriminating, and confidential information, and to present apologia.

IV. *Written Questionnaires*

The *questionnaire* as a means of eliciting information and opinions is not altogether a recent innovation. Many generals, for instance (Washington is a good example), required their staff officers to submit written answers to a series of questions on strategy, and rulers or prime ministers often did likewise with cabinet officers on questions of policy. Where the questionnaire is intended, as in such instances, to elicit present opinion only, it is highly reliable as a source of such opinion, particularly if the questions are precise, the answers properly weighted, and the confidential relationships between questioner and questioned assured. Where, however, it is intended to extract information about the experience of the person questioned, it is likely to be somewhat unreliable. Let us suppose a well-trained educator filling out a precise questionnaire on his own early education as carefully as he can. This, it will readily be admitted, is a rare combination of circumstances favorable to credibility. Yet the answers would be not only subject to all the strictures that have been made regarding personal bias and memory lapses; they would also be suspect of all the evils of the "leading question." If the same educator had been asked to describe his earlier education in a single, uncircumscribed narrative, it is quite probable that his distribution of emphasis and his silences would have been different and more revelatory of the truth.

Yet such questionnaires will undoubtedly uncover much information not otherwise available.[13] Moreover, questionnaires now frequently try to overcome the disadvantages inherent in the "leading question" by allowing room for "comments" or "remarks." The historian of the medieval universities would pawn his typewriter and travel to the most remote and isolated archives to examine such questionnaires if they were to be found there, for, let us say, the University of Bologna in the twelfth century. If he is sometimes less enthusiastic about efforts that may, if only as a by-product, provide the future historian of the twentieth century with parallel documents, it is because their questions are not only "leading questions" but often misleading and "loaded," or because too great claims are made as to what they signify. Witness some recent "public opinion polls" and reports on "the American male," which in fact were polls of some groups and reports on some males only, although probably highly reliable ones for those who were in fact polled and reported upon.

V. *Government Documents and Compilations*

Many historians have altogether too respectful an attitude toward *government documents and compilations* and this deference is shared by some political scientists and sociologists. What has already been said about *official histories* (pp. 103–4) ought to be re-

---

[13] Cf. L. V. Koos, *The Questionnaire in Education, a Critique and Manual* (New York, 1928).

called. It should never be forgotten that many kinds of *government documents* often are not even primary sources. To be sure, statistics — vital, actuarial, census, fiscal — are frequently available nowhere but in government publications and therefore have to be derived from them or not at all. Yet the responsible editor upon whose authority they ultimately rest was probably not the compiler, and the compiler probably had to depend upon enormous staffs of less responsible persons — perhaps even temporarily employed and sometimes remarkably inexpert census-takers, surveyors, examiners, or assessors. Some kinds of governmental publications, therefore, are not in fact primary sources at all but are compilations from reports of many compilers, perhaps several steps removed from the actual observation. Yet when they are reports of *the proceedings of governmental bodies* or *laws and regulations* they may very properly be considered firsthand. Government compilations are apt to differ from records in the important regard that the farther their publication is from the origin of the the things compiled, the more reliable they are likely to be. The lapse of time may permit corrections of earlier compilations, greater care in making the compilation, and improvement of methods of acquiring the pertinent data, and probably also diminishes the political pressures upon the compilers.

(A) If the *proceedings of governmental bodies* are truly *stenographic* or *phonographic records*, they are to be treated as suggested above (p. 92). Too often, however, such proceedings are subject to doubt regarding their dependability as records. (1) Sometimes

they are made up long after the event. Striking examples are the first volumes of the *Moniteur* and the
whole of the *Archives parlementaires*. The *Moniteur*,
which eventually became the semi-official journal of
the French Revolutionary assemblies, actually began
only in November 1789. Later on, compilers went
back and made up the numbers from May to November. The *Archives parlementaires*, which purport
to be the debates of the French legislative assemblies
for 1789 to 1860 — with some gaps, however — were
actually prepared during the Second Empire. (2)
Even when *proceedings* appear more or less contemporaneously, they may contain "insertions." The *Con-
gressional Record*, in which members of Congress may
insert "speeches" that were never actually delivered,
is a crying example of that abuse of historical accuracy. (3) Most often the proceedings, though otherwise reliable, have been "polished" at least for style
and precision if not for contents. To the historian
interested in the mental life of the participants, such
manipulation of *proceedings* is a deprivation. It makes
confusion seem calm, conflict seem polite, and indeci-
sion seem deliberate, where excitement, bad manners, and planlessness would be nearer the truth. In
general, where reports of debates, whether in public
bodies or elsewhere, indicate that the debaters spoke
in smooth, grammatical, and finished sentences, it
may be taken for granted that they read their statements or polished them after delivery for publication,
although there are notable examples of speakers who
can deliver *ex tempore* remarks in sentences that
parse. When *government documents* are compiled,

polished, or supplemented in the ways indicated, they may be original (in the sense of being the earliest available) without necessarily being primary sources.

(2) *Laws and regulations* may seem to be totally impersonal documents at first glance, but a moment's thought reveals that they are the expression of the hopes, fears, commands, threats, or expectations of some individual or group of individuals. When the well-known financier, Lord Stamp, his wife, and his son Wilfred were killed in April, 1941, by a German bomb which fell on their home in Kent, the House of Lords decided that the son had outlived the father by a single second, though there were no surviving witnesses. If Wilfred had been first to die, his heirs would have had no right to Lord Stamp's title. The Lords' decision was an expression of their wish that Wilfred's widow and daughters might be recognized as holding titles by virtue of the alleged momentary survival of their husband and father.[14] When the laws of Soviet Russia prohibit anti-semitism, that does not mean that anti-semitism does or does not exist in Russia so much as it denotes the wish of someone to wipe it out wherever it may exist. The laws of Calvin's Geneva, which punished sexual immorality with fearful penalties, were perhaps less an indication of social behavior in Geneva than a revelation of Calvin's social philosophy. It is true, however, that official compilations of *laws and regulations* are primary evidence of their own content; they are only inferential evidence of the motives and feelings behind them.

---

[14] *New York Times*, October 9, 1941.

VI. *Expressions of Opinion*

Editorials, essays, speeches, pamphlets, letters to the editor, public opinion polls, and the like are valuable to the historian of opinion, whether individual or public. For their statements of fact, they may or may not be reliable, depending upon the competence of their authors as witnesses. Even as expressions of opinion, questions regarding their sincerity arise, and it must be corroborated by other evidence. Such documents are frequently, however, the best sources of the opinion expressed available to the historian.

A word of caution is made necessary by the temptation to believe that agreement among many opinions establishes as fact the point agreed upon. If thousands of Praxiteles' contemporaries said that he was a good sculptor and only a few that he was a bad one, that would be merely a poll of opinion proving what the majority of the individuals consulted thought but not proving that Praxiteles was a good sculptor. Even a most systematic *public opinion poll* would establish at best the degree of consensus on the question polled among those represented by the sample polled and not the correctness of the opinions given or of the factual data implied in the consensus.

To discover how good Praxiteles or any other artist was is perhaps not a "historicable" problem. One would have first to define what qualities make a good artist and then to discover to what degree the artist in question possessed those qualities. The second point would probably still have to be ascertained largely by *expressions of opinion* rather than testimony of observations. Even if such opinion and testimony were carefully compiled and discounted, there would still be room for dispute as to whether the definition of the requisite qualities of a "good sculptor" had been correct to begin with, and as to whether the correct proportion of each quality had entered into the definition. Such problems in aesthetics can easily be paralleled in ethics. And "value judgments" like these are, as we shall see (pp. 243–5), the very soul of history for some historians. Even those historians who are the most dryly "scientific" confess that human frailty makes it difficult for the historian to avoid pronouncing judgments regarding the good, the true, and the beautiful. But if such pronouncements can be proved at all, they certainly cannot be established by adding up contemporary opinions.

In fact, there is a school of historians who contend that values and ideas change with periods of history, that what is a justifiable principle of aesthetics, morality, or politics at one time may be less so at another, that thought patterns are relative to contemporary conditions arising out of the cultural and historical climate of a given area and time. That belief, which would deny the validity of absolute principles or of a single system of truthful interpretation in history, is sometimes called *objective relativism* or *historical relationism*. It is a by-product of the nineteenth-century development called *historicism*, which we shall discuss again in Chapter X. *Historicism*, in reaction to those who maintain that truth and the meaning of life are to be found only in God or Reason or the Law of Nature or the Absolute, maintains that they are to be

found in History. It insists upon the relation of ideas
to historical circumstances (including other ideas); it
maintains that ideas are only "reflex functions of the
sociological conditions under which they arose." [15]
"Objective relativism" is closely akin to the sociology
of knowledge (*Soziologie des Wissens*). It is largely
a German school of thought. It stems from Hegel and
Marx through Weber, Dilthey, and Troeltsch to
Meinecke and Mannheim.

It should be pointed out, however, that Troeltsch
and Mannheim both insist that their brand of historicism does not include a crude historical *relativism*,
which they distinguish from *relationism* and repudiate
as denying all concept of carry-over and totality. *Relativism* is likely to imply indifference to enduring
ethical and aesthetic standards. It carries a connotation of misjudgment due to personal idiosyncrasies
and ephemeral pressures from which the judge has
not made the proper effort to detach himself rather
than a connotation of coloration due to cultural conditions, "climates of opinion," and "frames of reference" that no man can fully escape. *Relationism* or
objective relativism seeks to know that set of standards which best characterizes a people or a period.
Thus historians of this school advocate the search for
a different kind of values — those that "objectively"
interpret the ideology of historical periods.[16]

---

[15] Karl Mannheim, "Troeltsch, Ernst," *Encyclopaedia of Social
Sciences*. Cf. Randall and Haines, "Controlling Assumptions in the
Practice of American Historians," Curti *et al.*, pp. 22–3.

[16] Ernst Troeltsch, *Christian Thought, Its History and Application*, ed. F. Von Hugel (London, 1923), pp. 105–06. Mannheim's
Ideology and Utopia (New York, 1936) is somewhat contradictory

VII. *Fiction, Song, and Poetry*

William Graham Sumner has made clear how important literary works may be to the American social scientist.[17] They have significance as documents to the historian in any capacity. (1) They reveal the author's likes and dislikes, hopes and fears. (2) They provide the historian with an understanding of some of the local color, the environment, that helped to shape the author's views. By way of illustration, much of our knowledge of social customs in Augustan Rome is derived from the poetry of Virgil, Horace, Ovid, and other contemporaries. When Chaucer tells us that the prioress of the *Canterbury Tales* spoke French after the school of Strattford-atte-Bowe though she knew no French of Paris, that she let not a morsel of food drop from her lips upon her breast nor wet her fingers in the

---

on this point. E.g., he states (p. 73) that "far from being permanently valid, the interpretation of culture in terms of objective values is really a peculiar characteristic of the thought of our times." Nevertheless, he later deliberately identifies himself with that type of "sociological approach to history" that forms "the first step in the direction which ultimately leads to an evaluative procedure and to ontological judgments" (p. 83). Friedrich Meinecke's *Ideengeschichte* likewise contains, along with a study of ideas as influenced by their own setting, the idea of "historical individuality" and the appreciation of values; cf. E. N. Anderson, "Meinecke's *Ideengeschichte* and the Crisis in Historical Thinking" in *Historical Essays in Honor of James Westfall Thompson* (Chicago, 1938), pp. 361–96, and C. A. Beard and Alfred Vagts, "Currents of Thought in Historiography," *American Historical Review*, XLII (1937), 466–7. See also below, pp. 219–20.

[17] *Folkways: A Study of the Sociological Importance of Usages, Manners, Customs, Mores and Morals* (Boston, 1907). Cf. Allport, pp. 113–4.

gravy bowl, that she carefully wiped her lips and left
no stain of grease upon her cup, we are informed not
only about Chaucer's standards of etiquette and dain-
tiness but also about Chaucer's England. When
Shakespeare has Othello exclaim:

> . . . O curse of marriage,
> That we can call these delicate creatures ours,
> And not their appetites! I had rather be a toad,
> And live upon the vapour of a dungeon,
> Than keep a corner in the thing I love,
> For other uses. . . .

both Shakespeare's and the Elizabethans' ideas of
marriage stand in some small part revealed. A large
work has been written on the manners of seventeenth-
century French largely from literary sources.[18]

Highly trained specialists in the so-called "sciences
auxiliary to history" have produced such amazing results that historians in fields in which these specialists
have worked are now no longer so dependent as they
once were upon merely literary sources. Epigraphers
have provided corpora of inscriptions taken from ancient monuments, tombs, animal bones, and clay tablets. Papyrologists have read the thoughts and words
preserved in the papyri of ancient Egypt. Paleogra-
phers have prepared printed texts of medieval charters
and manuscripts now hardly legible except to the experts. Still the historians of social behavior, attitudes,
and cultural patterns of ancient Chinese, Biblical,

---

[18] Maurice Magendie, *La Politesse mondaine et les théories de
l'honnêteté en France au xviie siècle de 1600 à 1660* (Paris, 1926).
Cf. also Max von Boehn, *Modes and Manners*, tr. Joan Joshua
(Philadelphia, 1932–6).

Greek, Roman, and medieval times have few sources better than the contemporary works of philosophy, fiction, drama, and poetry. Usually, however, the historian does not dare to use the information these works contain unless it is confirmed by other knowledge. For until he knows the locality well, he has no way of ascertaining whether the local color has the proper shade.

VIII. *Folklore, Place Names, and Proverbs*

That is especially true of folklore. The stories of William Tell, legendary hero of the Swiss war of independence, and Dr. Faustus, sixteenth-century necromancer, are good examples of folklore that may tell much about the aspirations, superstitions, and customs of the peoples among whom the stories developed, provided the historian (or folklorist) is able to distinguish between the legendary embroideries and their authentic foundations. The same may be said of the world's great sagas and myths, whether crystallized into Homeric epics or holy scripture. Folk rhymes have a similar historical value. It may very easily be true that "the butcher, the baker, the candlestick maker" were members of some of the most powerful guilds in medieval England and that Little Jack Horner was a land-grabbing noble of Henry VIII's court, but the folklorist who discovers such things is aided by his knowledge of history more than he aids the historian. Place names are nearly in the same category. Names like Bath or Aix or Aachen may help locate ancient watering-places; the generous spread of French names in North American geography may help to illustrate the enterprise of French explorers and settlers in the seventeenth and eighteenth centuries, but they may also be recently acquired. Certain proverbs may reveal indigenous mores rather than borrowings, but alone they are only indications of possibilities. Unfortunately, for many historical developments in remote times we have no more than such feeble indications.

Interrelationship of Document and Setting

In short, proverb, folklore, and place names, as well as fiction, song, and poetry, need a historical setting to be useful to the historian. But that is true of historical documents in general, whether fiction or non-fiction, whether intentionally or unintentionally prepared for examination by the historian. While it undoubtedly is true that they largely reflect the cultural atmosphere of their times (*Zeitgeist*, "climate of opinion," milieu), the historian who does not already know those particular times thoroughly cannot tell to what extent the documents are influenced by, conflict with, or exerted influence upon that cultural atmosphere. The *Zeitgeist* must therefore be studied in order fully to understand any contemporary document; and yet it is also true that the documents of a period will enable the historian better to appreciate its cultural atmosphere.

Secondary Sources

The historian often has to depend upon secondary works (i.e., other historians' second-hand narratives and expositions) for his knowledge of the background into which to fit the contemporary documents, but he frequently also finds that, just as a good secondary account will enable him better to understand a contemporary document, so the correct understanding of the contemporary document will enable him to correct the secondary account. In the end, his knowledge is best tested by a critical analysis of the testimony of contemporaries.

Hence, as a general rule, the careful historian will be suspicious of secondary works in history, even the best ones. He should use them only for four purposes: (1) to derive the setting into which to fit the contemporary evidence upon his problem, being always prepared, however, to doubt and to rectify the secondary account wherever a critical analysis of contemporary witnesses makes it necessary to do so; (2) to get leads to other bibliographical data; (3) to acquire quotations or citations from contemporary or other sources, but only if they are not more fully available elsewhere and always with skepticism about their accuracy, especially if they are translated from another tongue; and (4) to derive interpretations of and hypotheses regarding his problem, but only with a view to testing or improving upon them, never with the intention of accepting them outright.

In general, the rule regarding time-lapse as applied to secondary sources is the reverse of that rule as applied to primary sources. The further away secondary sources are in time from the events of which they tell, the more reliable they are likely to be. That is true not only because impartiality and detachment are easier for remote periods of history, but also because as time elapses, more materials are likely to become available. In addition, the last writer has the help of the materials and interpretations contained in the earlier studies of his subject. Unfortunately, later historians are not always as competent as earlier ones. All too frequently they are just hack-writers, content merely with "re-hashing" the earlier works without presenting new evidence or points of view.

CHAPTER VI

THE PROBLEM OF AUTHENTICITY, OR EXTERNAL CRITICISM

So far it has been assumed that the documents dealt with have been authentic. The problem of authenticity seldom concerns the sociologist or psychologist or anthropologist, who generally has a living subject under his eye, can see him as he prepares his autobiography, and can cross-examine him about doubtful points. Even in the law courts the question of authenticity of documents becomes a difficult problem only on rare occasions, when the writer or witnesses to the writing cannot be produced.[1] But for historical documents those occasions are not rare. They are in fact frequent for manuscript sources; and if doubt as to authenticity arises less often for printed sources, it is because usually some skilled editor has already performed the task of authenticating them.

Forged or Misleading Documents

Forgeries of documents in whole or in part without being usual, are common enough to keep the careful historian constantly on his guard. "Historical documents" are fabricated for several reasons. Sometimes they are used to bolster a false claim or title. The classic example is the Donation of Constantine, which

---

[1] Wigmore, pp. 326–36.

formed a basis of the papal claim to a wide jurisdiction in the west. In 1440 Lorenzo Valla proved, chiefly by means of anachronisms of style and allusion, that it had been forged. At other times documents are counterfeited for sale. Counterfeit letters of Queen Marie Antoinette used to turn up frequently.[2] A Philadelphia autograph dealer named Robert Spring once manufactured hundreds of skillful forgeries in order to supply the demand of collectors. A recent notorious example of forgery was the "correspondence" of Abraham Lincoln and Ann Rutledge, palmed off on the *Atlantic Monthly* in 1928.

Sometimes fabrication is due to less mercenary considerations. Political propaganda largely accounts for the Protocols of the Elders of Zion, a "document" pretending to reveal a ruthless Jewish conspiracy to rule the world.[3] Sometimes historical "facts" are based only on some practical joke, as in the case of H. L. Mencken's much cited article on the "history" of the bathtub, or of Alexander Woollcott's mocking letter of endorsement of Dorothy Parker's husband (of which he never sent the original to the supposed addressee, although he did send the carbon copy to the endorsee).[4] The *Mémoires* of Madame d'Epinay are a striking ex-

---

[2] Lord Acton, *Lectures on the French Revolution* (London, 1910), pp. 361–4.

[3] See J. S. Curtis, *An Appraisal of the Protocols of Zion* (New York, 1942).

[4] Cf. C. D. MacDougall, *Hoaxes* (New York, 1940), pp. 302–9; Dorothy Parker, reviewing A. *Woollcott: His Life and His World* by S. H. Adams (New York, 1945) in the *Chicago Sun Book Week* of June 10, 1945.

ample of fabrication of a whole book that has beguiled even respectable historians.[5]

Sometimes quite genuine documents are intended to mislead certain contemporaries and hence have misled subsequent historians. A statement supposed to be that of Emperor Leopold II's views on the French Revolution misled Marie Antoinette and subsequently even the most careful historians until it was exposed in 1894 as a wishful statement of some French émigrés.[6] In days when spies were expected to open mail in the post, writers of letters would occasionally try to outwit them by turning their curiosity to the advantage of the one spied upon rather than to that of the spy or his employer.[7] And when censors might condemn books to be burned and writers to be imprisoned, authors could hardly be blamed if they sometimes signed others' names to their work. For instance, it is hard to tell whether some works actually written by Voltaire are not still ascribed to others. It is thus possible to be too skeptical about a document which may be genuine though not what it seems. Bernheim has provided a list of documents that were once hypercritically considered unauthentic but are now accepted.[8] Perhaps it was hypercriticism of this

---

[5] The "cheating document" is discussed with a wealth of absorbing detail in Allan Nevins, *Gateway to History* (Boston, 1938), ch. V, pp. 119–37.

[6] Acton, *French Revolution*, p. 119.

[7] Cf. Lafayette to William Carmichael, March 10, 1785, quoted in Louis Gottschalk, *Lafayette between the American and the French Revolution* (Chicago, 1950), pp. 156–7.

[8] Ernst Bernheim, *Lehrbuch der historischen Methode und der Geschichtsphilosophie* (6th ed.; Leipzig, 1908), pp. 376–91.

kind that led Vincent Starrett to write his verse entitled "After Much Striving for Fame":

> It would be rather jolly, I think,
> To be the original authority
> On some obscure matter of literature or faith
> Upon which, in one's leisure,
> One had jotted down an inaccurate pamphlet;
> And forever thereafter
> To be quoted by all post-Vincentian borrowers
> In a pertinacious footnote.[9]

Occasionally misrepresentations of the nature of
printed works result from editors' tricks. It is still
a matter of dispute which of the many writings attributed to Cardinal Richelieu were in fact written or
dictated by him; and little of the so-called *Mémoires
de Jean de Witt* and *Testament politique de Colbert*
were in fact written by John de Witt and Colbert.
The memoirs attributed to Condorcet and to Weber,
foster-brother of Marie Antoinette, and several works
ascribed to Napoleon I are by others than their alleged authors. Even issues of daily newspapers have
been manufactured long after the dates they bear.
The *Moniteur* furnishes some good examples (see
p. 107 above). Several *Diaries* of Napoleon have been
made up by others from his writings. The circumstances of the forgery or misrepresentation of historical documents may often themselves reveal important political, cultural, and biographical information —
but not about the same events or persons as if they
were genuine.

---

[9] Quoted by permission of Mr. Starrett.

Tests of Authenticity

To distinguish a hoax or a misrepresentation from a genuine document, the historian has to use tests that are common also in police and legal detection. Making the best guess he can of the *date* of the document (see below pp. 138 and 147–8), he examines the *materials* to see whether they are not *anachronistic*: paper was rare in Europe before the fifteenth century, and printing was unknown; pencils did not exist there before the sixteenth century; typewriting was not invented until the nineteenth century; and India paper came only at the end of that century. The historian also examines the ink for signs of age or for anachronistic chemical composition. Making his best guess of the possible *author* of the document (see below pp. 144–7), he sees if he can identify the handwriting, signature, seal, letterhead, or watermark. Even when the handwriting is unfamiliar, it can be compared with authenticated specimens. One of the unfulfilled needs of the historian is more of what the French call "isographies" — dictionaries of biography giving examples of handwriting. For some periods of history, experts using techniques known as *paleography* and *diplomatics*, first systematized by Mabillon in the seventeenth century (see p. 127 below), have long known that in certain regions at certain times handwriting and the style and form of official documents were more or less conventionalized. *Seals* have been the subject of special study by sigillographers, and experts can detect faked ones (see below, p. 128). *Anachronistic style* (idiom, orthography, or punctuation) can be detected by specialists who are familiar with contemporary writing.[10] Often spelling, particularly of proper names and signatures (because too good or too bad or anachronistic), reveals a forgery, as would also unhistoric grammar. *Anachronistic references to events* (too early or too late or too remote) or the dating of a document at a time when the alleged writer could not possibly have been at the place designated (the *alibi*) uncovers fraud. Sometimes the skillful forger has all too carefully followed the best historical sources and his product becomes too *obviously a copy* in certain passages; or where, by skillful paraphrase and invention, he is shrewd enough to avoid detection in that fashion, he is given away by the *absence of trivia and otherwise unknown details* from his manufactured account.[11] Usually, however, if the document is where it ought to be — for example, in a family's archives, or among a business firm's or lawyer's papers, or in a governmental bureau's records (but not merely because it is in a library or in an amateur's autograph collection) — its *provenance* (or its *custody*, as the lawyers call it),[12] creates a presumption of its genuineness.

---

[10] Cf. Marcel Cohen, "Comment on parlait le français en 1700," *L'Europe*, XXV (1947), 18–23.

[11] Cf. *They Knew the Washingtons; Letters from a French Soldier with Lafayette and from His Family in Virginia*, tr. Princess Radziwill (Indianapolis, 1926); and Henri Béraud, *My Friend Robespierre*, tr. Slater Brown (New York, 1928).

[12] *Wigmore*, pp. 330–1.

Garbled Documents

A document that in its entirety or in large part is the result of a deliberate effort to deceive may often be hard to evaluate, but it sometimes causes less trouble than does the document that is unauthentic only in small part. For such parts are usually the result, not of studied falsehood, but of unintentional error. They occur most frequently in copies of documents whose originals have disappeared, and are generally due to that kind of error of omission, repetition, or addition with which anyone who has ever made copies soon becomes familiar. Sometimes they are the result, however, not of carelessness but of deliberate intention to modify, supplement, or continue the original. Such a change may be made in good faith in the first instance, care being exerted to indicate the differences between the original text and the glossary or continuations, but future copyists are often less careful or more confused and make no such distinctions.

This problem is most familiar to classical philologists and Bible critics. For they seldom have copies less than eight centuries and several stages of reproduction removed from the original — that is to say, copies of copies of copies, and sometimes copies of translations of copies of translations of copies, and so on. The philologists give to this problem of establishing an accurate text the name *textual criticism*, and in Biblical studies it is also called *lower criticism*. The historian has borrowed his technique from philologists and Bible critics.

The Restoration of Texts

The technique is complicated but can be briefly described. The first task is to collect as many copies of the dubious text as diligent research will reveal. Then they are compared. It is found that some contain words or phrases or whole passages that are not contained in others. The question then arises: Are those words, phrases or passages additions to the original text that have found their way into some copies, or are they omissions from the others? To answer that question it is necessary to divide the available copies into one or more "families" — that is, groups of texts which closely resemble each other and therefore seem to be derived, directly or indirectly, from the same master copy. Then by a comparison of the texts within each family an effort is made to establish the comparative age of each in relation to the others. If the members of the same family are largely copied from each other, as this arrangement in families frequently shows, the oldest one is in all probability (but not necessarily) the one nearest the original. This process is continued for all the families. When the copy nearest the original in each family is discovered, a comparison of all of these "father" copies will usually then reveal words and passages that are in some but not in others. Again the question arises: Are those words and passages additions to the copies that have them or omissions from the copies that do not? The most accurate available wordings of the passages added or omitted by the respective copyists are then prepared. Changes in handwritings, anachronisms in style, grammar, orthography, or factual detail, and opinions or errors unlikely to have been those of the original author frequently reveal additions by a later hand. When the style and contents of passages under discussion may be attributed to the author, it is safe to assume that they were parts of his original manuscript but were omitted by later copyists; and when they cannot be attributed to the author, it is safe to assume that they were not parts of his original manuscript. In some cases, a final decision has to await the discovery of still more copies. In many instances the original text can be approximately or entirely restored.

By a similar method one can even guess the contents, at least in part, of a "father" manuscript even when no full copy of it is in existence. The historian Wilhelm von Giesebrecht, a student of Ranke, attempted to reconstruct a text that he reasoned must be the ancestor of several eleventh-century chronicles in which he had noted striking similarities. By adding together the passages that appeared to be "descended" from an unknown chronicle, he made a guess as to its contents. Over a quarter of a century later the ancestor chronicle was in fact found, and proved to be extensively like Giesebrecht's guess.

Sciences Auxiliary to History

The problem of textual restoration does not frequently disturb the present-day historian, chiefly because many experts, engaged in what the historian egocentrically calls "sciences auxiliary to history," provide him with critically prepared texts. Since Jean François Champollion in 1822 first learned to decipher hieroglyphics, part of the work of *Egyptologists and papyrologists* has been to provide the historian with texts and translations of inscriptions and papyri found in the ancient Nile Valley, whether in Egyptian hieroglyphic or in cursive hieratic and demotic or in Greek. The *Assyriologists*, since Sir Henry Rawlinson in 1847 deciphered Old Persian cuneiform and in 1850 Babylonian cuneiform, have been publishing and translating the texts found on the clay tablets of the ancient Tigris-Euphrates civilizations. Biblical criticism, even before Erasmus, was directed to the effort of bringing the text of both the Old and the New Testament as close as possible to the original wording and of explaining as fully as possible the Hebrew and Hellenistic civilizations which they reflected. *Philology*, as already explained, deals among other things with the derivation from variant texts of the most authentic ones (especially of classical literature). The *classical epigrapher* restores and edits the texts of Greek and Latin inscriptions found on the gravestones, monuments, and buildings of ancient Greece and Rome. The *paleographer*, since the time that Mabillon (see p. 122) first formalized the principles of *paleography and diplomatics*, has been able to authenticate medieval charters and other documents by their handwritings, which have been found to vary from place to place and from time to time, and by their variant but highly stylized conventions and forms, and to publish easily legible printed versions of them. The *archeologist* excavates ancient sites and provides the historian with information derived from artifacts such as statues, mausoleums, pottery, buildings, and building materials. The *science of numismatics* has enabled the numismatist to authenticate and date coins and metals and to decipher and explain their inscriptions. *Sphragistics* (or *sigillography*) has done the same thing with regard to seals, and in so doing has provided an additional test for the authenticity of the documents whose seals they authenticate. The sciences of *heraldry* and *genealogy* authenticate coats of arms and lines of descent, and genealogists put forth dictionaries of genealogy and genealogical tables. The *bibliographer* furnishes information with regard to books and authors, provides bibliographies, catalogues, and dictionaries of authors, authenticates incunabula, first editions, and rare items, detects hoaxes, and identifies anonymities. The *lexicographer* prepares dictionaries of words, gives their derivation, and the history and examples of their variant usages; much interesting historical knowledge will disappear if lexicographers should ever fail to record the derivation of numerous words like *bonfire, chauvinism, china, boycott, lynch,* and *macadamize* (which will repay looking up in the dictionary). Of late, social scientists such as the *educationist,* the *anthropologist,* the *psychologist,* and the *sociologist* have been publishing questionnaires, public opinion polls, statistics on populations and social change, etc. Conclusions obtained from such materials and so-called "personal documents" or autobiographies collected by social scientists have been or will be useful to the historian. So long as the historian's work deals with printed materials prepared by skillful specialists in "the sciences auxiliary to history" he is saved from the gravest dangers of the historical hoax or the garbled document. He may analyze their publications on the cheerful assumption that they are authentic as documents, and he need only determine the credibility of their contents.

Chronology as an Auxiliary Science

The study of *chronology* simplifies for the historian the vital problem of time measurement. The chronologist clarifies the various calendars that have been in use in different places at different times and makes it possible to translate datings from one calendar into the others. This is no simple task, because there have been so many different ways of reckoning time in the world's history. Even when western Europe was religiously united under the Catholics and widely accepted the (erroneously dated) birth of Jesus as a zero point from which to count time forward and backward, various localities celebrated New Year's day on different dates and so, for part of the year at least, did not agree as to what year it was. Pope Gregory XIII in the sixteenth century, reformed the curious mixture of Egyptian, Roman, and Christian reckonings used till then and known as the "Julian Calendar," and brought it into greater conformance with the latest astronomical knowledge. But by that time Christendom was split into Greek Orthodox, Catholic, and Protestant fractions, and his reform at first prevailed only in the Catholic countries. Protestant countries adopted it one by one. In the British possessions it was not accepted until 1752, when the Old Style of dating was eleven days behind the Gregorian (or New Style) calendar, and when from January 1 to March 24 the Old Style Calendar was one year earlier, because it reckoned the new year as not beginning until March 25. That is why we celebrate Washington's birthday as of February 22, 1732, although his family Bible records it as of February 11, 1731. The countries under Orthodox influence did not generally accept the Gregorian calendar until the twentieth century, when their Old Style calendar was thirteen days behind the Gregorian. That explains why the Bolshevik revolution of 1917 is still referred to as the "October Revolution" although the Russians celebrate its anniversary on what is now November 7.

At least two common errors can be avoided by bearing in mind that the Gregorian calendar contains no year 0. The first century A.D. ran from the year 1 to the year 100, and the nineteenth century from 1801 to 1900; and the twentieth century will run from 1901 to 2000. Hence the first half of the nineteenth century did not end until midnight, December 31, 1850 (not 1849), and the same holds true for earlier centuries as well as for our own. For the same reason a calculation of the lapse of time between a year B.C. and a year A.D. requires subtraction of 1 from their sums. Thus, the lapse of time between 1 B.C. and A.D. 1 was not two years (more or less) but one year (more or less), and that between 63 B.C. and A.D. 14 (the dates of Augustus) would be 76 years (not 77).

All Christendom and many other peoples under Western influence now use the Gregorian calendar, but some non-Christian peoples (e.g., the Moslems and the Israeli) still use calendars derived from their independent religious traditions. The attempt of the French Revolutionary assemblies to adopt a scientific calendar encountered religious opposition and failed (unlike their reform of weights and measures by the introduction of the metric system). The preparation of concordances for the different styles of reckoning time is the business of the chronologist. He also provides tables and thesauri of persons and events with dates in order to make "the art of verifying dates" simpler.

Variants Among the Sources

Often, the historian runs into two or more different texts of the same document published by responsible experts. And in modern history, where thousands of archives and libraries, and the stacks, vaults, and filing-cases of lawyers, courts, doctors, psychoanalysts, business firms, social agencies, autograph collectors and dealers, families, kings, presidents, governors, ministries, legislatures, armies, navies, committees, churches, schools, teachers, county and municipal officials, tax and police authorities, newspapers, clubs, academies, lodges, commissions, etc. are crammed with unpublished documents, he sometimes comes upon two or more manuscript or typewritten copies of the same document that are not identical. The blockade by the English of the American coast during the American War of Independence necessitated sending three or four copies of important letters from America to France and those copies did not always agree in detail. In the warehouses full of paper on the Second World War, there are bound to be several drafts or copies of the same document that nevertheless will show discrepancies. In such instances the historian has to try, like the philologist, to determine which copy is the nearest to the original in time; that usually makes it easier to determine additions and omissions and thus to explain the discrepancies.

Sometimes, too, published versions are incorrect, and comparison with the original manuscript is required.[13] More often paraphrases and descriptions of the sources are faulty. One must always remember the lesson of the heresy trial of Professor G. B. Foster of the University of Chicago Divinity School. When he was brought up before an ecclesiastical conference on the charge of having called those who believed in the Bible *knaves*, it was found by reference to the proper page in his book that what he had in fact said was, "He who calls himself a Bible believer is a *naive*." [14] No less astute a person than the Russian diplomat Andrei Vishinsky in 1948 announced before the United Nations that an American map existed of "the Third World War, Pacific theatre of military operations," but reference to the map itself revealed it was entitled "War Map III Featuring the Pacific

---

[13] For example, the published version of an important document in the so-called "Conway cabal" rendered as "tho he" words that were in the original "Mr. Lee," thus long obscuring the part Francis Lightfoot Lee played in the "cabal." See Louis Gottschalk, *Lafayette Joins the American Army* (Chicago, 1937), p. 120 and n. Cf. Louis Gottschalk and Josephine Fennell, "Duer and the 'Conway Cabal,'" *American Historical Review*, LII (1946), 87–96.

[14] Wigmore, pp. 219–20.

Theatre." It was nothing more than the third map relating to the war (the first two were of the European theatre) published by a certain American map company during the Second World War.[15]

The Problem of Meaning: Semantics

Having procured as nearly accurate a text as his sources will provide, the historian is then faced with the task of determining its meaning. This is the problem that in Biblical criticism is called *hermeneutics* and *exegesis*. It sometimes involves the varying signification of words — or semantics. Such problems may call only for the use of a dictionary, but that means, wherever possible, lexicons contemporary to the author of the document or, at least, a dictionary arranged on historical principles; for the meanings of words often change from generation to generation. The words *liberty* and *right* seldom mean more than *privilege* in feudal documents; and the word *proletarian* meant little more than *vile* or *vulgar* before the nineteenth century. *Imperialist* was a more laudatory term in the 1880's than in the 1950's; and today *democracy* changes meaning as one travels east or west of the Oder River. Failure to realize such changes in meaning may lead to thorough misunderstanding of important historical developments.

The semantic problem also involves the exploitation of all the knowledge that the historian possesses concerning the period and the witness. For frequently witnesses, particularly illiterate ones, do not use dic-

---

[15] *New York Times*, October 3, 1948, reproduces the front page of the map.

tionary words, or use dictionary words in senses and in combinations not authorized by the dictionaries. Moreover, failure to appreciate the intellectual climate in which the witness lived may make words conveying his aspirations, superstitions, or other ideas lose some of their overtones. Knowing that witches are real to some people, that the divine intervention of the gods is no less real to others, that devils, imps, and fairies inhabit various worlds, that private property is sacred to some and anathema to others, that God saves some by inner grace and others by good works, that miracles are signs of holiness to some and of credulity to others — knowing such patterns of thought and hundreds more like them, contradictory or supplementary, enables the historian of each era to grasp nuances that might otherwise escape him. The historian's task is to understand not only what a document's words may formally mean but also what his witness *really intended to say*.

The Problem of Meaning: Hermeneutics

When one encounters language that is ambiguous, an additional query arises since the ambiguity might or might not have been accidental. What, for example, did the man mean who wrote to an author, "I shall lose no time reading your book"? Did he mean that the book was well worth reading, or that it would be a waste of time to read it and he therefore would not do so, or that he would hasten to read it? And was the ambiguity unintentional? If, as is sometimes said, the man was the cynical Benjamin Disraeli, it probably was not, but without any context one might assume the remark was intended to be polite though unhappily phrased.

The hermeneutic problem becomes especially acute when a deliberate intention to hide the meaning is suspected. The deliberate hiding of meaning involves not merely the problem of code and cypher and the danger of reading one's prejudices into a document; [16] it involves also a certain amount of skill with riddles, puzzles, and word-tricks. The *New York Times*, shortly after the 1940 invasion of France, published an octave (translated below) which, appearing originally in *Paris-Soir*, seemed to indicate some Frenchman's great admiration for Hitler and contempt for the English:

> Aimons et admirons le Chancelier Hitler
> L'éternelle Angleterre est indigne de vivre;
> Maudissons et écrasons le peuple d'outremer;
> Le Nazi sur la terre sera seul à survivre.
> Soyons donc le soutien du Fuehrer allemand,
> Des boys navigateurs finira l'odyssée;
> A eux seuls appartient un juste châtiment;
> La palme du vainqueur attend la Croix Gammée.

But any historian would have been thoroughly deceived as to its meaning and purport, and therefore as to the writer's and publisher's traits and attitudes, if he had taken it at its face value. For these are Alexandrine verses, and by separation on the caesura, two stanzas of eight lines each are produced that have an altogether opposite meaning, as the *Times's* translation showed:

---

[16] Cf. M. R. Cohen and Ernest Nagel, *An Introduction to Logic and Scientific Method* (New York, 1934), pp. 329–34.

With love let us praise
Everlasting England
Let us curse, let us raze
On earth, the Nazi band
Let us then bear support
For the boys plowing the
        sea
By whose sole effort
The victory shall be

Hitler, the Chancellor,
Is unworthy of life,
The trans-Channel mentor —
Sole survivor in strife —
For the German Chieftain

Shall the Odyssey fade,
Just punishment obtain,
For the Swastika glaive.

Historical-Mindedness

Closely related to the semantic and hermeneutic problem is that of understanding and appreciating behavior in its contemporary setting. To judge earlier societies by more advanced codes of ethics; to expect balanced judgments and normal conduct in times of war, revolution, or upheaval; to translate the folkways, conventions, and standards of one country to another; to condemn an individual's act without attempting to comprehend his norms or environment; to be intolerant of an "ignorance" which is in fact a comprehensive knowledge of and a healthy adjustment to a different culture — these and other failures to place persons and events in their own historical setting would often lead to failure to understand the surviving documents and nearly always to misjudgments of the personalities and *mores* of that setting.

The ability to put oneself in the place of other individuals of other times and to interpret documents, events, and personalities with their eyes, standards, and sympathies (without necessarily surrendering one's own standards) has sometimes been called *his-*

torical-mindedness. It is closely related to the processes psychologists call *empathy* and *intuition*. It requires a deliberate effort to control and to correct another skill that, while of a similar nature, may easily work in an opposite direction — the ability to interpret the past in terms of *analogy* to one's experience (see below, pp. 272–7). While a historian's questions about any earlier period that he studies are more or less bound to arise from his own present — his own frames of reference, standards, institutions, situations, traditions, and aspirations, nevertheless he has the obligation as a historian to answer them in terms of his subject's situations and "ecology."

Historical-mindedness requires the investigator to shed his own personality and to take on, as far as possible, that of his subject in the effort to understand the latter's language, ideals, interests, attitudes, habits, motives, drives, and traits. This may be hard to do and the historian may rarely succeed in doing it thoroughly, but the obligation upon him is obvious if he is attempting to understand and impartially judge rather than to criticize others' acts and personalities. Historical-mindedness sometimes requires the historian to make a better case for a subject than the subject could have made for himself, without necessarily believing it. He should put into his personality studies something of the understanding, but not necessarily forgiving, quality that a psychiatrist might give to the study of a patient. This is much the same kind of understanding that Acton admired in George Eliot's character portrayals: "Each of them should say that she displayed him in his strength, that she gave rational form to motives he had imperfectly analyzed, that she laid bare features in his character he had never realized." [17] If Morris R. Cohen is right, "To widen our horizon, to make us see other points of view than those to which we are accustomed, is the greatest service that can be rendered by the historian, and this he can do best by concentrating on the special field which he studies to understand." [18]

Identification of Author and of Date

Some guess of the approximate date of the document and some identification of its supposed author (or, at least, a surmise as to his location in time and space and as to his habits, attitudes, character, learning, associates, etc.) obviously form an essential part of *external criticism*. Otherwise it would be impossible to prove or disprove authenticity by anachronisms, handwriting, style, alibi, or other tests that are associated with the author's milieu, personality, and actions. But similar knowledge or guesses are also necessary for *internal criticism*, and therefore the problem of author-identification has been left for the next chapter (pp. 144–8).

Having established an authentic text and discovered what its author really intended to say, the historian has only established what the witness's testimony is. He has yet to determine whether that testimony is at all credible, and if so, to what extent. That is the problem of *internal criticism*.

[17] January 21, 1881, Herbert Paul (ed.), *Letters of Lord Acton to Mary Gladstone* (New York, 1904), p. 159.

[18] *The Meaning of Human History* (La Salle, Ill., 1947), p. 28.

CHAPTER VII

THE PROBLEM OF CREDIBILITY,
OR INTERNAL CRITICISM

THE HISTORIAN first aims in the examination of testimony to obtain a set of particulars relevant to some topic or question that he has in mind. Isolated particulars have little meaning by themselves, and unless they have a context or fit into a hypothesis they are of doubtful value. But that is a problem of *synthesis,* which will be discussed later.[1] What we are now concerned with is the *analysis* of documents for credible details to be fitted into a hypothesis or context.

What Is Historical Fact?

In the process of *analysis* the historian should constantly keep in mind the relevant particulars within the document rather than the document as a whole. Regarding each particular he asks: Is it credible? It might be well to point out again that what is meant by calling a particular *credible* is not *that it is actually what happened,* but that it is *as close to what actually happened as we can learn from a critical examination of the best available sources.*[2] This means *verisimilar* at a high level. It connotes something more than merely *not being preposterous in itself* or even than *plausible* and yet is short of meaning *accurately de-*

---

[1] See Chapter IX.
[2] Cf. above pp. 45-9.

scriptive of past actuality. In other words, the historian establishes *verisimilitude* rather than *objective truth*. Though there is a high correlation between the two, they are not necessarily identical. As far as mere particulars are concerned, historians disagree relatively seldom regarding what is *credible* in this special sense of "conforming to a critical examination of the sources." It is not inconceivable that, in dealing with the same document, two historians of equal ability and training would extract the same isolated "facts" and agree with each other's findings. In that way the elementary data of history are subject to *proof*.

A historical "fact" thus may be defined as a particular derived directly or indirectly from historical documents and regarded as credible after careful testing in accordance with the canons of historical method (see below p. 150). An infinity and a multiple variety of facts of this kind are accepted by all historians e.g., that Socrates really existed; that Alexander invaded India; that the Romans built the Pantheon; that the Chinese have an ancient literature (but here we introduce a complexity with the word *ancient* which needs definition before its factual quality can be considered certain); that Pope Innocent III excommunicated King John of England; that Michelangelo sculptured "Moses"; that Bismarck modified Kaiser William I's dispatch from Ems; that banks in the United States in 1933 were closed for four days by presidential proclamation; and that "the Yankees" won the "World Series" in 1949. Simple and fully attested "facts" of this kind are rarely disputed. They are easily observed, easily recorded (if not self-evident

like the Pantheon and Chinese literature), involve no
judgments of value (except with regard to the an-
tiquity of Chinese literature), contradict no other
knowledge available to us, seem otherwise logically
acceptable, and, avoiding generalization, deal with
single instances.

Even some apparently simple and concrete statements, however, are subject to question. If no one
disputes the historicity of Socrates, there is less agreement regarding Moses and earlier figures of Hebrew
folklore. If no one doubts that Michelangelo sculptured
his "Moses," a few still think that Shakespeare's plays
were in fact written by Francis Bacon. Doubt regarding concrete particulars is likely to be due, however,
to lack of testimony based on first-hand observation
rather than to disagreement among the witnesses. In
general, on simple and concrete matters where testimony of direct observation is available, the testimony
can usually be submitted to tests of reliability that
will be convincing either *pro* or *con* to most competent
and impartial historians. As soon as abstractions, value
judgments, generalizations, and other complexities enter into testimony the possibility of contradition and
debate enters with them. Hence, alongside the multitude of facts generally accepted by historians, exists
another multitude debated (or at least debatable) by
them.

The Interrogative Hypothesis

In analyzing a document for its isolated "facts,"
the historian should approach it with a question or
a set of questions in mind. The questions may be rela-

tively noncommittal. (E.g.: Did Saul try to assassi-
nate David? What were the details of Catiline's life?
Who were the crusading companions of Tancred?
What was the date of Erasmus' birth? How many
men were aboard De Grasse's fleet in 1781? What is
the correct spelling of Sieyès? Was Hung Hsui-chu'an
a Christian?) It will be noted that one cannot ask
even simple questions like these without knowing
enough about some problem in history to ask a question about it, and if one knows enough to ask even
the simplest question, one already has some idea and
probably some hypothesis regarding it, whether implicit or explicit, whether tentative and flexible or
formulated and fixed. Or the hypothesis may be full-
fledged, though still implicit and in interrogative
form. (E.g.: Can the Jews be held responsible for
the crucifixion of Jesus? Did the medieval city develop from the fair? Why did the Anabaptists believe
in religious liberty? How did participation in the
American Revolution contribute to the spread of liberal ideas among the French aristocracy? Why did
Woodrow Wilson deny knowledge of the "secret
treaties"?) In each of these questions a certain im-
plication is assumed to be true and further clarification of it is sought on an additional working assumption.

Putting the hypothesis in interrogative form is more
judicious than putting it in declarative form if for
no other reason than that it is more noncommittal
before all the evidence has been examined. It may also
help in some small way to solve the delicate problem
of relevance of subject matter (see pp. 196–201 be-

low), since only those materials are relevant which lead directly to an answer to the question or indicate that there is no satisfactory answer.

The Quest for Particular Details of Testimony

As has already been pointed out, every historical subject has four aspects — the biographical, the geographical, the chronological, and the occupational or functional. With a set of names, dates, and key-words in mind for each of these aspects, the historical investigator combs his document for relevant particulars (or "notes," as he is more likely to call them). It is generally wise to take notes on relevant matter whether or not it at first appears credible. It may turn out that even false or mistaken testimony has relevance to an understanding of one's problem.

Having accumulated his notes, the investigator must now separate the credible from the incredible. Even from his "notes" he has sometimes to extract still smaller details, for even a single name may reveal a companion of Tancred, a single letter the correct spelling of *Sieyès*, a single digit the exact number of De Grasse's crew, or a single phrase the motives of Wilson's denial. In detailed investigations few documents are significant as a whole; they serve most often only as mines from which to extract historical ore. Each bit of ore, however, may contain flaws of its own. The general reliability of an author, in other words, has significance only as establishing the probable credibility of his particular statements. From that process of scrupulous analysis emerges an important general rule: *for each particular of a docu-*

ment the process of establishing credibility should be separately undertaken regardless of the general credibility of the author.

Identification of Author

As has already been pointed out (p. 138), some identification of the author is necessary to test a document's authenticity. In the subsequent process of determining the credibility of its particulars, even the most genuine of documents should be regarded as guilty of deceit until proven innocent. The importance of first establishing the author's general reliability is therefore obvious. Where the name of the author can be determined and he is a person about whom biographical data are available, identification is a relatively easy task. Because, in most legal and social science investigations, the witness or the author of a document is personally known and available to the investigator, that question generally presents no insurmountable difficulties to lawyers and social scientists.

The historian, however, is frequently obliged to use documents written by persons about whom nothing or relatively little is known. Even the hundreds of biographical dictionaries and encyclopedias already in existence may be of no help because the author's name is unknown or, if known, not to be found in the reference works. The historian must therefore depend upon the document itself to teach him what it can about the author. A single brief document may teach him much if he asks the right questions. It may, of course, contain explicit biographical details, but to assume that would be begging the question. Even where it is relatively free from first-person allusions, much may be learned of the author's mental processes and personal attitudes from it alone.

Let us take the usual text of Lincoln's Gettysburg Address, and assume for the sake of example that we have no knowledge of it except for what its own contents may reveal:

Fourscore and seven years ago our fathers brought forth on this continent a new nation, conceived in liberty, and dedicated to the proposition that all men are created equal. Now we are engaged in a great civil war, testing whether that nation, or any nation so conceived and so dedicated, can long endure. We are met on a great battlefield of that war. We have come to dedicate a portion of that field, as a final resting-place for those who here gave their lives that that nation might live. It is altogether fitting and proper that we should do this. But, in a larger sense, we cannot dedicate — we cannot consecrate — we cannot hallow — this ground. The brave men, living and dead, who struggled here, have consecrated it, far above our poor power to add or detract. The world will little note, nor long remember, what we say here, but it can never forget what they did here. It is for us the living, rather, to be dedicated here to the unfinished work which they who fought here have thus far so nobly advanced. It is rather for us to be here dedicated to the great task remaining before us, — that from these honored dead we take increased devotion to that cause for which they gave the last full measure of devotion — that we here highly resolve that these dead shall not have died in vain — that this nation, under God, shall have a new birth of freedom — and that government of the people, by the people, for the people, shall not perish from the earth.

Even a hasty examination will suffice to make clear that the author, at the time of writing, was planning to use it as a speech ("we are met," "what we say here"), that he wrote English well, that his address was a funeral oration ("we have come to dedicate a portion of that field as a final resting place"), that he was probably a prominent citizen, that he presumably was an American ("our fathers," "this continent," "new nation," "four score and seven years ago"), that he was an advocate of liberty and equality (or at least desired his hearers to think so), that he lived during the American Civil War, that he was speaking at Gettysburg, or possibly Vicksburg ("great battlefield," "four score and seven years ago"), and that he wanted his side in the war to be thought of as fighting for democracy ("government of the people, by the people, for the people"). If we forget the controversy among historians as to whether the words *under God* were actually delivered or were only afterward inserted, we may assume that he subscribed, or wished to appear to subscribe, to the belief in a Supreme Being.

From a short document, it would thus appear, it is possible to learn much about the author without knowing who he was. In the case of the Gettysburg Address a trained historian would probably soon detect Lincoln's authorship, if it were unknown. But even if he had never heard of Lincoln, he would be able to tell that, in attempting to judge the truth of the particulars stated in that address, he would have to consider it as probably a public exhortation by a prominent antislavery Northerner after a major victory over the Confederate States in the American Civil War. Many documents, being less modest and less economical of words than the Gettysburg Address, give their authors away more readily.

Determination of Approximate Date

It would be relatively easy, even if the Gettysburg Address were a totally strange document, to establish its approximate date. It was obviously composed "four-score and seven years" after the Declaration of Independence, hence in 1863. But few strange documents are so easily dated. One has frequently to resort to the conjectures known to the historian as the *terminus non ante quem* ("the point not before which") and the *terminus non post quem* ("the point not after which"). These *termini*, or points, have to be established by internal evidence — by clues given within the document itself. If the date 1863 were not implicit in the Gettysburg Address, other references within the speech could point obviously to the beginning of the American Civil War as its *terminus non ante quem*, and since the war was obviously still going on when the document was composed, its *terminus non post quem* would be the end of the Civil War. Hence its date could be fixed approximately, even if the first sentence had been lost, as somewhere between 1861 and 1865; and if we were enabled by other data to guess at "the great battlefield," we might even narrow that margin. Some documents might not permit even a remote guess of their termini, but where the author is known, one has at least the dates of his birth and death to go by.

The Personal Equation

This analysis of the Gettysburg Address (under the false assumption that its authorship is unknown) indicates the type of question the historian asks of both anonymous and avowed documents. Was the author an eyewitness of the events he narrates? If not, what were his sources of information? When did he write the document? How much time elapsed between the event and the record? What was his purpose in writing or speaking? Who were his audience and why? Such questions enable the historian to answer the still more important questions: Was the author of the document *able* to tell the truth; and if able, was he *willing* to do so? The ability and the willingness of a witness to give dependable testimony are determined by a number of factors in his personality and social situation that together are sometimes called his "personal equation," a term applied to the correction required in astronomical observations to allow for the habitual inaccuracy of individual observers. The personal equation of a historian is sometimes also called his "frame of reference," but it probably will be found more expedient to restrict the latter term to his conscious philosophy or philosophies of life in so far as they can be divorced from personality traits and biases of which he may or may not be aware.

General Rules

In a law court it is frequently assumed that all the testimony of a witness, though under oath, is suspect if the opposing lawyers can impugn his general character or by examination and cross-examination create doubt of his veracity in some regard. Even in modern law courts the old maxim *falsus in uno, falsus in omnibus* tends to be overemphasized.[3] In addition, hearsay evidence is as a general rule excluded;[4] certain kinds of witnesses are "privileged" or "unqualified" and therefore are not obliged to testify or are kept from testifying;[5] and evidence obtained by certain means regarded as transgressing the citizen's rights — such as "third degree," drugs, wire-tapping, or lie-detector — are ruled out of some courts. The legal system of evidence, says James Bradley Thayer, "is not concerned with nice definitions, or the exacter academic operations of the logical faculty. . . . Its rules . . . are seeking to determine, not what is or is not, in its nature, probative, but rather, passing by that inquiry, what among really probative matters, shall, nevertheless, for this or that practical reason, be excluded, and not even heard by the jury."[6] Courts of law, in the Anglo-Saxon system at least, go on the assumption that if one side presents all the permissible testimony in its favor and if the other side presents all the permissible testimony in its, the truth

---

[3] Wigmore, p. 181.

[4] Ibid., pp. 238–45.

[5] Ibid., pp. 125–34 and 354–60.

[6] *Preliminary Treatise on Evidence at the Common Law* (Boston, 1896), pp. 3–4.

will emerge plainly enough for judge and jury from the conflict or harmony of the testimony, even if some kinds of testimony are not permissible; and possibly where much and recent testimony is available, the innocent suffer less often by such an assumption than the guilty escape.

The historian, however, is prosecutor, attorney for the defense, judge, and jury all in one. But as judge he rules out no evidence whatever if it is relevant. To him any single detail of testimony is credible — even if it is contained in a document obtained by force or fraud, or is otherwise impeachable, or is based on hearsay evidence, or is from an interested witness — provided it can pass four tests:

(1) Was the ultimate source of the detail (the primary witness) *able* to tell the truth?

(2) Was the primary witness *willing* to tell the truth?

(3) Is the primary witness *accurately reported* with regard to the detail under examination?

(4) Is there any *independent corroboration* of the detail under examination?

Any detail (regardless of what the source or who the author) that passes *all four* tests is credible historical evidence. It will bear repetition that the *primary witness* and the *detail* are now the subjects of examination, not the source as a whole.

Ability to Tell the Truth

(1) Ability to tell the truth rests in part upon the witness's nearness to the event. *Nearness* is here used in both a geographical and a chronological sense. The

reliability of the witness's testimony tends to vary in proportion to (a) his own remoteness from the scene in time and space, and (b) the remoteness from the event in time and space of his recording of it. There are three steps in historical testimony: observation, recollection, and recording (not to mention the historian's own perception of the witness's record). At each of these steps something of the possible testimony may be lost. Geographical as well as chronological closeness to the event affects all three steps and helps to determine both how much will be lost and the accuracy of what is retained.

(2) Obviously all witnesses even if equally close to the event are not equally competent as witnesses. *Competence* depends upon degree of expertness, state of mental and physical health, age, education, memory, narrative skill, etc. The ability to estimate numbers is especially subject to suspicion. The size of the army with which Xerxes invaded Greece in 480 B.C. was said by Herodotus to have numbered 1,700,000, but it can be shown to have been considerably less by the simple computation of the length of time it would have taken that many men to march through the Thermopylae Pass even unopposed. More recently by a similar computation doubt was thrown upon the veracity of a newspaper report from Moscow that one million men, women, and children paraded through the Red Square in celebration of the thirty-second anniversary of the October Revolution (November 7, 1949) in a five and one-half hour demonstration, for it would require more than fifty persons a second to march abreast past a given point to com-

plete a parade of one million in five and one-half hours.[7] With some notable exceptions, such as the *Domesday Book* of William the Conqueror, historians have been warned against using any source of numbers before the end of the Middle Ages.[8] The careful keeping of vital statistics was a relatively late innovation of the end of the eighteenth and the beginning of the nineteenth century. Previous to that time tax rolls and incomplete parish records of baptisms, marriages, and burials were the best indications. Even battle casualty statistics before the nineteenth century are suspect, and historians still disagree on the cost in human life of wars up to and including those of Napoleon I, and, in some instances, beyond.

(3) *Degree of attention* is also an important factor in the ability to tell the truth. A well-known story, no less illustrative if it be apocryphal, tells of a psychology professor who deliberately staged a fight in his classroom between two students, which led to a free-for-all. When peace was restored, the professor asked each member of the class to write an account of what had happened. There were, of course, conflicting statements among the accounts, but, what was most significant, no student had noticed that the professor in the midst of the pandemonium had taken out a banana and had peeled and eaten it. Obviously the entire meaning of the event rested upon the unno-

---

[7] Letter of John E. Frazer, November 9, 1949, *New York Times*, November 15, 1949.

[8] Seignobos, *Méthode historique appliquée aux sciences sociales*, pp. 204–5.

ticed act; it was an experiment in the psychology of attention. Because each student's interest had been fixed upon his own part in the drama, each had given an erroneous interpretation of what had occurred. Magicians similarly depend upon their ability to divert attention from things they are doing to perpetrate some of their tricks. The common human inability to see things clearly and whole makes even the best of witnesses suspect.

(4) We have already discussed the danger of the *leading question* (p. 104). Such questions, by implying the expected answer, make it difficult to tell the whole truth. Lawyers also count the *hypothetical question* ("Supposing you did agree with me, would you act as I?"), and the *argumentative or "loaded" question* ("Have you stopped beating your wife?"), and the *coached answer* as belonging to kindred categories.[9] Such questions are especially liable to be misleading if they have to be answered "Yes" or "No." Allport gives a striking illustration of the kind of misinformation that can be derived from the witness whose narrative is circumscribed by the questioner. He mentions an investigator who "secured fifty topical autobiographies, forcing all writers to tell about radicalism and conservatism in their lives," and who from those biographies almost (but fortunately not quite) came to the conclusion that "radicalism-conservatism constitutes one of those first-order variables of which all personalities are compounded."[10]

(5) In the last instance the investigator barely

---

[9] Cf. Wigmore, pp. 147–50 and 160–2.

[10] Allport, p. 137.

missed *reasoning in a circle* — from premise back to premise again. It has been contended also that one of the reasons why religious problems and events receive so much attention in the history of the Middle Ages is that its principal sources were written by clergymen. If medieval architects, landowners, soldiers, or merchants had written more, they might have asked and answered different kinds of questions and given a different picture of medieval life. Possibly, if the writings of our own intellectuals should prove to be the major source for future accounts of our age, future historians will be misled into thinking that intellectuals had a greater influence upon human affairs in our time than they actually have. This sort of circular argument must be especially guarded against when an effort is being made to ascribe unsigned writings to a supposed author, for it is easy to assume that the ideas of the writings are characteristic of the supposed author if those very articles are the basis of the assumptions regarding the author's characteristics.

(6) One almost inescapable shortcoming of the personal document is its *egocentrism*. It is to be expected that even a modest observer will tell what he himself heard and what he himself did as if those details were the most important things that were said and done. Often it is impossible for him to tell his story in any other terms, since that is the only way he knows it. This observation is a more or less inevitable corollary of the caution with regard to *attention* discussed above. The famous speech of the Comte de Mirabeau after Louis XVI's Royal Session of June 23, 1789, provides a pat illustration of how

easily such egocentrism may mislead the historian. Mirabeau (though speaking in the third person) told how he had said something about the necessity of force: "For we shall leave our seats only by the power of the bayonet." He failed to mention that several others were expressing a similar determination at about the same time, though probably in more moderate language. Therefore historians trusting too confidently to Mirabeau's testimony have sometimes made him the heroic center of a desperate crisis; still it is more probable that he was not so conspicuous or the situation so dramatic as he implied.[11]

In general, *inability to tell the truth* leads to errors of omission, rather than commission, because of lack of completeness or lack of balance in observation, recollection, or narrative. Such errors may give a picture that is out of perspective because it subordinates or fails to include some important things and overemphasizes those it does include.

Willingness to Tell the Truth

The historian also has to deal with documents whose authors, though otherwise competent to tell the truth, consciously or unconsciously tell falsehoods. There are several conditions that tend especially toward untruthfulness and against which the experience of mankind has armed lawyers, historians, and others who deal with testimony.[12]

---

[11] Cf. F. M. and H. D. Fling, *Source Problems of the French Revolution* (New York, 1913), p. 129; cf. also pp. 123, 139, 144, and 148.

[12] Wigmore, pp. 176–90.

(1) One of the most elementary rules in the analysis of testimony is that which requires the exercise of caution against the *interested witness*. A witness's interest is obvious when he himself may benefit from perversion of the truth or may thereby benefit some one or some cause dear to him. Certain kinds of *propaganda* are perhaps the worst examples of deliberate perversion of truth out of a desire to benefit a cause. In the seventeenth century the word *propaganda* was applied to Catholic missionary work without disparagement. Since the nineteenth century, however, it has been used more or less derogatorily to designate any kind of concerted movement to persuade and the instruments of such persuasion. The word may be modern, but propaganda and its methods have been familiar since efforts were first made to influence public opinion.

(2) Often the benefit to be derived from a perversion of the truth is subtle and may not be realized by the witness himself. In such a case the cause of prevarication probably is *bias*. If the witness's *bias* is *favorable* to the subject of his testimony, it is frequently designated *studium*. If it is *unfavorable*, it may be designated *odium* or *ira*. The Latin words are derived from a declaration by Tacitus that he would write history *sine studio et ira* (thereby setting a standard that few historians, including Tacitus, have been able to achieve). *Studium* and *odium*, bias for and bias against, frequently depend upon the witness's social circumstances and may operate in a fashion of which he himself may not be aware. It becomes important to the historian to know what the

witness's *Weltanschauung* (or "frame of reference") may be, as well as his religious, political, social, economic, racial, national, regional, local, family, personal, and other ties (or "personal equation"). Any of these factors may dictate a predilection or a prejudice that will shade his testimony with nuances that otherwise might have been absent.

(3) The intended hearers or readers of a document, it has already been remarked (p. 90), play an important part in determining the truthfulness of a statement. The *desire to please or to displease* may lead to the coloring or the avoidance of the truth. Speakers at political rallies and at banquets, writers of wartime dispatches and communiqués, makers of polite letters and conversation are among the numerous producers of documents that may subtly pervert fact for that reason. Akin to and often associated with *interest* and *bias*, which are often socially determined, this motive is nevertheless different from them, being usually personal and individual. It may occasionally stand alone as an explanation of prevarication.

(4) *Literary style* sometimes dictates the sacrifice of truth. Epigrams and — notoriously — slogans of war and politics ("*L'état c'est moi*"; "Millions for defense but not one cent for tribute"; "The Old Guard dies but never surrenders"),[13] if properly discredited in the interests of accuracy and truthful reporting, would be robbed of pithiness and color. Authors of autobiographies and letters, especially when they write

---

[13] Paul Harsin, *Comment on écrit l'histoire* (Paris, 1933; English adaptation, Berkeley, 1935) contains an appendix that cites a number of other examples with critical analysis of their origin.

for private amusement, may feel tempted to state as fact what is only hearsay or tradition or even fiction; and frequently narrators and reporters (especially if they hope for large audiences) seek to appear omniscient rather than to use the less vigorous word, the less striking phrase, the *ifs* and *buts*, the *there-is-some-reason-to-believe* and the *it-is-perhaps-safe-to-say* of more precise discourse (but see also pp. 186–7 below).

The anecdote is especially suspect. Much too often it is a subsequent invention to throw into humorous or striking relief some spectacular figure or episode. The more apposite the anecdote, the more dubious it is likely to be without corroboration. And yet the existence of an especially pat anecdote has a historical significance of its own — as showing the sort of thing believed of or imputed to the subject. A well-known Italian proverb describes such anecdotes as felicitous (*ben trovato*) even if untrue.

(5) *Laws and conventions* sometimes oblige witnesses to depart from strict veracity. The same laws of libel and of good taste that have encouraged the hiding of the "resemblance to persons now living or dead" in fiction and moving pictures have precluded complete accuracy in some works of history. Some of the notorious inaccuracies of Jared Sparks as a historian were due to his writing of living characters from testimony by living witnesses who requested him not to use certain data.[14] Etiquette in letters and conversation, conventions and formalities in treaties and public documents require politeness and ex-

---

[14] Louis Gottschalk, *Lafayette and the Close of the American Revolution* (Chicago, 1942), p. 252.

pressions of esteem that are obviously false or empty. A successful comedy, James Montgomery's *Nothing but the Truth* (1916), was written around the valiant effort of a young man to go through a whole day without saying anything that was untrue; it nearly cost him all his friends. Religious taboos like the Christian Scientist's avoidance of the ideas of *evil*, *disease*, and *death* may lead to misapprehension. Corporations, commissions, and societies are sometimes required by their articles of incorporation or constitutions to meet periodically, but when their numbers are small, the minutes of their meetings may be much more formal than the actual meetings.

(6) Closely akin to this category are the many instances of *inexact dating* of historical documents because of the conventions and formalities involved. For example, the official text of the Declaration of Independence is dated "In Congress, July 4, 1776." To the unwary reader it would appear that those who signed it were present and did so on that day. In fact, the formal signing took place on August 2, 1776, and some members did not sign until a still later date.[15] Some medieval rulers used to date documents as of certain towns though they were not at those towns on the dates indicated. The modern official's and businessman's habit of sending letters on office stationery regardless of where they may be or of dictating but not reading their letters, which are signed by a rubber stamp or a secretary, may make it very difficult for future biographers to trace their itineraries.

---

[15] Carl Becker, *Declaration of Independence* (New York, 1922), pp. 184-5.

Bank checks, having the city of the bank's location printed on them, may also prove misleading as to the signer's whereabouts.

(7) *Expectation or anticipation* frequently leads a witness astray. Those who count on revolutionaries to be bloodthirsty and conservatives gentlemanly, those who expect the young to be irreverent and the old crabbed, those who know Germans to be ruthless and Englishmen to lack humor generally find bloodthirsty revolutionaries and gentlemanly conservatives, irreverent youth and crabbed old-age, ruthless Germans and humorless Englishmen. A certain lack of precision is found in such witnesses because their eyes and ears are closed to fair observation; or because, seeking, they find; or because in recollection, they tend to forget or to minimize examples that do not confirm their prejudices and hypotheses. (This sort of attitude is only a special kind of *bias* and might be regarded merely as a subdivision of Paragraph 2 above.)

* * *

Unwillingness to tell the truth, whether intentional or subconscious, leads to misstatements of fact more often than omissions of fact. When the same witness is both unable and unwilling to tell the truth (as is mostly the case to some degree at least), the historian has before him a document that commits errors both of omission and commission. Yet he must continue to bear in mind that even the worst witness may occasionally tell the truth and that it is the historian's business to extract every iota of relevant truth, if he can.

Conditions Favorable to Credibility

Fortunately there are certain conditions especially favorable to truthfulness, and students of evidence easily recognize them. They are frequently the reverse of the conditions that create an inability or an unwillingness to tell the truth.

(1) When the purport of a statement is a matter of indifference to the witness, he is likely to be unbiased.

(2) More dependably, when a statement is prejudicial to a witness, his dear ones, or his causes, it is likely to be truthful. That is why confessions, if not forcibly extracted and if deposed by those in good mental health, are considered excellent testimony, sometimes acceptable in law courts without other direct testimony.[16] The historian must be careful, however, to make sure that the statement really is considered by the witness to be prejudicial to himself. Cases like that of Charles IX's claim of responsibility for the St. Bartholomew Massacre, Bismarck's satisfaction with his revision of the Ems dispatch, and ex-Nazis' or ex-Communists' contrition over their youthful errors come all too readily to mind. In such cases the deponent may be engaged in a subtle and perhaps unconscious form of self-pity or even of boasting rather than in confession, and other tests of trustworthiness must be sought.

(3) Often, too, facts are so well-known, so much *matters of common knowledge*, that the witness would be unlikely to be mistaken or to lie about

---

16 Wigmore, pp. 305–6.

them: viz., whether it rained last night, whether a prominent citizen was assassinated last Tuesday, whether a famous bishop was a notorious philanderer, whether a well-known lord had the largest herd of sheep in the county, etc. Whenever the implications of such testimony suggest that such matters are common knowledge — and especially when they are also commonplaces — the absence of contradictory evidence in other sources may frequently be taken to be confirmation. For example, it is a commonplace that old soldiers are grumblers, and, besides, many persons had abundant chance to observe this phenomenon in particular armies; hence we are prepared to believe the tradition that many of Napoleon's veterans were *grognards* even on otherwise inadequate testimony. If that kind of statement had been incorrectly reported, it would in all probability have been challenged by other contemporaries writing subsequently.

This process of reasoning rests, however, upon a sort of *argumentum ex silentio* ("Silence gives consent"), and such arguments can easily be abused. Care must be taken to ascertain whether, though apparently commonly known or commonplace, the matter under examination was in fact so regarded by other contemporaries, and whether they ever had a chance to learn of and to contradict the earlier testimony. In times of panic, for instance, it is easy to exaggerate the number of enemies of the state, and the very existence of the panic may lead to silence on the part of those who do not share it. Where, on the other hand, there is any reason to believe a matter extraordinary, though commonly known, the argument from silence would work the other way: the very fact that a statement of something extraordinary was not corroborated in other sources that might have been expected to mention it would render it suspect. The ambivalence of the *argumentum ex silentio* makes it a weak test for most purposes. It is not the silence of other possible witnesses but whether an event was considered commonplace or extraordinary that lends credibility to or removes credibility from single statements on matters of common knowledge.

(4) Even when the fact in question may not be well-known, certain kinds of statements are *both incidental and probable* to such a degree that error or falsehood seems unlikely. If an ancient inscription on a road tells us that a certain proconsul built that road while Augustus was princeps, it may be doubted without further corroboration that that proconsul really built the road, but it would be harder to doubt that the road was built during the principate of Augustus. If an advertisement informs readers that "A and B Coffee may be bought at any reliable grocer's at the unusual price of fifty cents a pound," all the inferences of the advertisement may well be doubted without corroboration except that there is a brand of coffee on the market called "A and B Coffee." Although the opinion that "William Jones' widow is a more charming lady than Mrs. Brown" may have no validity as testimony regarding the relative merits of the two ladies, it is probably good evidence on the physical condition of William Jones.

Even the boldest propaganda may be made to yield credible information by a careful application of the

rule regarding *the incidental and the probable*. Such
a statement in a propaganda leaflet as: "Our aircraft
easily overcame the enemy's," would be, without confirmation from more reliable sources, thoroughly suspect with regard to the inferiority of the enemy. Yet
it may be taken at its face value as evidence that the
enemy have airplanes (especially since it is not only
incidental and probable but also *contrary to interest*
in that regard). And the statement may also have some
value as evidence that "we" have airplanes (though
that value is not as great as if the evidence were here
also *contrary to interest*). When in a war or a diplomatic controversy one side takes the trouble to deny
the propaganda of the other, neither the propaganda
nor the denial may be certified thereby, but it becomes clear that the propaganda has seemed worthy
of some attention to the other side.

(5) When the thought patterns and preconcep-
tions of a witness are known and yet he states something out of keeping with them — in other words, if
statements are *contrary to the witness's expectations
or anticipations*, they have a high degree of credibility.
Thus, a statement by a Soviet observer regarding instances of working-class contentment in a capitalist
country or by a capitalist observer regarding instances
of loyalty in a Soviet country would be especially impressive.

It must always be remembered that the skillful liar
can sense these conditions favorable to credibility as
well as most historians. Hence he can manufacture
an air of credibility that may easily take in the unwary
investigator. The existence of conditions favorable to

credibility such as these must first be established and never taken for granted in any given instance.

Hearsay and Secondary Evidence

The historian, let us repeat, uses *primary* (that is, *eyewitness*) testimony whenever he can. When he can find no primary witness, he uses the best secondary witness available. Unlike the lawyer, he wishes to discover as nearly as possible what happened rather than who was at fault. If he sometimes has to make judgments, he does not have to pass sentence and hence he does not have the same hesitation as a judge to permit evidence that practice has ruled out of courtrooms.

In cases where he uses secondary witnesses, however, he does not rely upon them fully. On the contrary, he asks: (1) On whose primary testimony does the secondary witness base his statements? (2) Did the secondary witness accurately report the primary testimony as a whole? (3) If not, in what details did he accurately report the primary testimony? Satisfactory answers to the second and third questions may provide the historian with the whole or the gist of the primary testimony upon which the secondary witness may be his only means of knowledge. In such cases the secondary source is the historian's "original" source, in the sense of being the "origin" of his knowledge. In so far as this "original" source is an accurate report of primary testimony, he tests its credibility as he would that of the primary testimony itself.

Thus hearsay evidence would not be discarded by the historian, as it would be by a law court, merely because it is hearsay. It is unacceptable only in so far as it cannot be established as accurate reporting of primary testimony. A single example will perhaps suffice to make that clear. A White House correspondent stating what the president had said at a press conference would be a primary source of information on the president's words. The same correspondent telling a presidential secretary's version of what the president had said would be a secondary or hearsay witness, and probably would be successfully challenged in a courtroom; and yet if the correspondent were a skilled and honorable reporter and if the presidential secretary were competent and honest, the correspondent's account might be a thoroughly accurate statement of what the president in fact had said. Even the most punctilious historian might retain that kind of evidence for further corroboration.

Corroboration

A primary particular that has been extracted from a document by the processes of external and internal criticism so far described is not yet regarded as altogether established as historical fact. Although there is a strong presumption that it is trustworthy, the general rule of historians (we shall soon note exceptions, however) is to accept as historical only those particulars which rest upon *the independent testimony of two or more reliable witnesses.*[17]

The importance of the *independence* of the wit-

---

[17] Cf. e.g., Bernheim, pp. 195–6 and 544; C. V. Langlois and C. Seignobos, *Introduction to the Study of History,* tr. G. G. Berry (London, 1912), pp. 199–205.

nesses is obvious. Independence is not, however, always easy to determine, as the controversy over the Synoptic Gospels well illustrates. Where any two witnesses agree, it may be that they do so because they are testifying independently to an observed fact, but it is possible that they agree only because one has copied from the other, or because one has been unduly influenced by the other, or because both have copied from or been unduly influenced by a third source. Unless the independence of the observers is established, agreement may be confirmation of a lie or of a mistake rather than corroboration of a fact.

It frequently happens, however, especially in the more remote phases of history, that diligent research fails to produce two independent documents testifying to the same facts. It is also evident that for many historical questions — the kind that would especially interest the student of biography — there often can be no more than one immediate witness. Of the emotions, ideals, interests, sensations, impressions, private opinions, attitudes, drives, and motives of an individual only that individual can give direct testimony, unless their outward manifestations are sufficiently well understood to serve as a reliable index. Even when those inner experiences are known from the testimony of others to whom the subject may have told them, they rest ultimately upon his own powers of introspection. The biographer is in this regard no better off than the psychologist — and worse off if his witness is dead and beyond interview. And all history is biographical in part. The biographer does, however, have one advantage over the psychologist — he knows what his subject is going to do next. He therefore can reason from response to sensation, from act to motive, from effect to cause. The completed behavior pattern may give confirmation to the biographer of the inward psychological processes of his subject.

It follows, then, that for statements known or knowable only by a single witness, we are obliged to break the general rule requiring two independent and reliable witnesses for corroboration. Hence we must look for other kinds of corroboration. A man's professed opinions or motives will seem more acceptable as his "honest" opinions or his "real" motives if they are not in keeping with the pattern of behavior that would be "fashionable" in the society in which he moved but at the same time are in keeping with what otherwise is known of his general character.[18] The very *silence* (i.e., absence of contradiction) of other contemporary sources upon a matter appearing to be common knowledge may sometimes be a confirmation of it (see above, p. 162). In other cases, a document's *general credibility* may have to serve as corroboration. The reputation of the author for veracity, the lack of self-contradiction within the document, the absence of contradiction by other sources, freedom from anachronisms, and the way the author's testimony fits into the otherwise known facts help to determine that general credibility.

Conformity or agreement with other known historical or scientific facts is often the decisive test of evidence, whether of one or of more witnesses. That

---

[18] Cf. F. H. Knight, "The Sickness of Liberal Society," *Ethics*, LVI (1946), 90–1.

Cellini saw fire-dwelling salamanders, devils, halos, and other supernatural phenomena would hardly seem credible to any modern historian, even if Cellini were otherwise generally truthful, consistent, and uncontradicted. And even if Cellini's statements were confirmed by independent witnesses, the historian would believe only that Cellini and his corroborators saw things they thought were salamanders, devils, and halos. General knowledge of how little effect a thumb in a hole in a dyke would have upon preserving a dyke that had begun to crumble would be sufficient to destroy credence in a well-known Dutch legend, even if there had been any witnesses to that hero's tale. Doubt can be thrown upon the old story that the potato was introduced into Ireland by Sir Walter Raleigh and hence to England by merely pointing to the fact that the Irish potato is of a different variety from the English potato.[19] What little we know about the time sequence of cause and effect induces us to believe that if notable contributions to anthropology appeared before and around 1859, the birth of modern anthropology cannot be said to be the result of the publication of Darwin's theory of evolution.[20] And, for obvious reasons, it is difficult to give much credence to a claim of virgin birth recently made in an English divorce case.

Because the *general credibility* of a document can rarely be greater than the credibility of the separate

---

[19] W. H. McNeill, "The Introduction of the Potato into Ireland," *Journal of Modern History*, XXI (1949), 219.

[20] Cf. F. J. Teggart, *Theory of History* (New Haven, 1925), pp. 105–6.

details in it, corroboration of the details of a witness's testimony by his general credibility is weak corroboration at best. Likewise the *argumentum ex silentio* and *conformity or agreement* with other known facts may be misleading. They are in the nature of *circumstantial evidence*, the weakness of which any reader of court proceedings and detective stories knows. While, in the cases under discussion, these tests are proposed only for *confirmation* of the direct testimony of one witness and not as exclusive sources of evidence, their circumstantial or presumptive nature renders them suspect even for that purpose. Hence historians usually insist that particulars which rest on a single witness's testimony should be so designated. They should be labeled by such tags as: "Thucydides says," "Plutarch is our authority for the statement that," "according to Suidas," "in the words of Erasmus," "if Boswell is to be believed," etc.

Certitude vs. Certainty

Since such precautions are not always taken and these single-witness statements are not always treated as *probanda* capable only of a lower order of proof, a curious paradox results. For many early periods of history, less disagreement is found among the sources, because there are fewer sources, than for more recent periods. On what happened one or two thousand years ago, despite the steady increase in archeological, epigraphical, papyrological, and paleographical materials, the sources are few, fairly generally available and known, and the contradictions among them relatively familiar if not always reconciled. On what happened last year, the sources are many and not always known, and the contradictions among them not yet familiar or reconciled. It is easier, among the enormous collections of little exploited or totally untapped materials on happenings of recent periods to find something unknown to describe or to reinterpret a familiar story on the basis of hitherto unused documents than to do either for events of remote periods. Hence, as a general rule, the more recent the period of study, the more difficult it becomes to say something that will remain long unchallenged; for both the intensity of controversy and the likelihood of a new approach tend to increase with the proximity in time to one's own day. Thus a greater degree of consensus and certitude may easily exist among historians where the testimony is lacking than where it is full. Perhaps nothing provides more eloquent proof than this that the historian's "truths" are derived from analytical evaluations of an object called "sources" rather than of an object called "the actual past."

CHAPTER VIII

LEARNING (AND TEACHING) HISTORICAL TECHNIQUES

Reasons for Studying History

ONE may decide to study history for many differer
reasons. Among them will be an idle curiosity abou
the past of one's family or one's locality, the urge t
explain to oneself the origins of one's culture, a pa
triotic interest in one's country's origin, the desire t
understand the social background and intellectual a
mosphere or to *chercher la femme* (or *l'homme*) of
great writer, artist, scientist, or leader whose work ha
aroused wonder or admiration, the hope that by un
derstanding the past development of a current prob
lem one may better understand its present implica
tions, a search for "the lessons of history" that wi
help contemporary man to solve his present problem
the wish to find in historical literature effective illu
trations for or checks upon an argument or a genera
ization, an absorption with some period of the pa
for its own sake, and the quest for a learned and ge
teel occupation. All these reasons may not be equal
commendable but none of them is likely to be repr
hensible, and the wise teacher of historical techniqu
will discourage none of them.

In learning historical method it is better for a st
dent to be impelled by his own interests than by th
teacher's. Nevertheless, wherever a choice seems po

ible, the teacher ought to apply pressure in the direction of the profound and abiding rather than of the
superficial and timely. Undismayed pursuit of the
right answers to the persistent questions is of greater
importance to society than definitive answers to questions that no longer matter. The persistent questions
may be raised, however, even in connection with local
affairs or obscure figures if the historian considers the
questions rather than the affairs or figures his major
interest.

The Usual Concept of History

The beginner is apt to think of historical research
as consisting of the selection of materials from several
books or articles and their rearrangement into another
book or article. Our usual system of historical training accustoms him to look upon some textbook or
anthology of sources and a set of "outside readings"
as "history." Even a "term paper" may not enable
him to acquire an appropriate sense of historical
method, since it generally requires no more than the
presentation in writing of a perhaps fuller selection
and a perhaps lengthier rearrangement in relation to
a perhaps more precise subject than he might otherwise undertake to prepare mentally from "the outside readings." Where that is true, it provides an exercise that differs from recitations, book reports, and
examinations based upon textbooks, source compilations, and assigned readings only physically and quan-
titatively rather than qualitatively. Hence the student in history classes is often only dimly aware that
history is also a method by which one endeavors to

find survivals and witnesses of some historical episod
about which one wishes to ask some question, to
collect all the relevant evidence they provide, and to
assess that evidence so as to arrive at some reliabl
answer.

Desirability of Encouraging the Student's Curiosity

If now the student is to be taught that historiog
raphy is something more than the rewriting in one'
own words of what has already been adequately se
forth in others' pages, he must first have some que:
tion of a historical nature that he would like to hav
answered. "Canned" questions such as "Who kille
Jesus?" "What were the relations of Franks and Gau
under Clovis?" "Was Robespierre benevolent or sel
seeking?" "What were the causes of the America
Civil War?" or "Was Germany responsible for th
outbreak of the First World War?" are not good on
for his purposes — not merely because they are so difl
cult as to have baffled mature scholars and divide
them into conflicting schools but also because the
moot quality has provided so vast a store of seconda
literature that a neophyte can hardly do more tha
read it, resting content with the old answers.

For the teaching of historical method, less im
portant questions to which he would really like t
know the answers are better than the graver ones t
which the world would like to know the answer
Hence, if he wishes to inquire about the past of som
local celebrity or some ancestor, if he wants to loc
further into some ancient crime or scandal, if he

inquisitive about the past statistics of his town, church, or country, if he is passionate about some past injustice to a minority group or some cause with which he identifies himself, or if he wishes to delve deeper into some mystery that has roused his intellectual curiosity, he should be encouraged to do so. He should, however, be warned early that while a trivial point of merely personal or antiquarian interest is excellent for demonstrating historical techniques, it is probably not the sort of question that will ultimately repay his effort, whether in terms of personal satisfaction, social import, or chances of publication. The danger of bias is enhanced, to be sure, the more the student identifies himself with his subject, but it is counterbalanced by his added zest for the search and his probably greater concern for the validity of his answer.

Helping a Student Select a Subject

Assuming, as in a goodly number of cases it is safe to assume, that the student will have no idea or only a vague one of what question to ask, the teacher can help him by remembering the fourfold aspect of any historical problem. He might ask what person or persons, what geographical area, what period of history, or what department of human endeavor interests the student most. In that way a beginner might be enabled to discover, perhaps for the first time, where his special interests lie.

By expanding or contracting the field of interest in the manner already explained (pp. 63–6), a question of manageable scope might be reached. Both teacher

and student ought to bear in mind the desirability
of avoiding at this stage certain kinds of questions:
(1) those involving value judgments; (2) contrasts
comparisons, and analogies; (3) causes, influences
and motivations; (4) questions involving indefinite
or debatable words like *instinct, race, atmosphere
spirit,* and *class*; and (5) questions connoting super
latives, like *all, never, first, most,* and *best* (which
usually without adding to the value of their answers
commit one to extensive investigations that more
elastic words permitting exceptions or oversight
would render unnecessary).

For teaching historical method at least, the more
precise and concrete a subject the better. For all it
faults, "What was the length of Cleopatra's nose?" i
a more appropriate subject than "Did the length o
Cleopatra's nose change the face of the world?"; and
the latter is better than "Was Pascal justified in think
ing, 'If Cleopatra's nose had been a little shorter
the whole face of the world would have been
changed'?" If the student had sufficient training in
the languages involved, he might conceivably find
some source that would enable him to decide whethe
Cleopatra's nose was normal, subnormal, or super
normal in size, or he could state that the evidenc
was not available. But an answer to the question rais
ing the importance of Cleopatra's nasal measure
ments to the world's history is a matter of judgmen
and is likely to differ with different philosophies o
history; and a judgment of Pascal would require som
knowledge of his philosophy and some ability with

iterary criticism besides. The beginner had better leave the face of the world to the Pascals.

To make sure that the student will also get training in the use of heuristical aids like catalogues, bibliographies, reference books, and current national book lists, he should be required to choose a subject that will involve the use of more than one source: not, for example, "What was Washington's opinion of slavery?" (which might well involve the use of only the collected writings of Washington) but rather 'What attitudes regarding slavery existed among Virginians in the 1780's?" To oblige the investigator to institute a search for all the available materials (using the secondary sources, however, only as indicated above, p. 116), it is desirable to limit the subject to so narrow a scope as to make a satisfying answer possible only after some minute research. Thus, "What attitude regarding slavery existed among Virginians in the 1780's?" might be limited to "What attitudes . . existed . . . in 1784?" or even "in June, 1784?" For, obviously, the more specialized a subject, (1) the less likelihood that the answer will be readily available in some secondary source, and (2) the greater likelihood that the student will be able to discover and control all the sources available to him within the time at his disposal. If students are also required to submit bibliographies of their subjects indicating the sources, both primary and secondary, that they actually examined and that they could not examine because they were not available, a further check on their use of bibliographical aids is provided (as well as a check on their understanding of the difference between primary and secondary sources). The subject can easily be expanded if necessary to include a greater area, longer time, more persons, or more activities if the number of sources should prove too few to keep the student profitably occupied.

Relevance of material, concreteness and precision of subject, and conciseness and coherence of composition can be further policed by an arbitrary limitation upon the size of the final report — for example, to the number of pages that can be intelligibly read aloud in twenty minutes or less. It is obviously better to have a direct, brief, and concise report than a long and rambling one if for no other reason than that correctness of method and logic of conclusion can be more readily judged when irrelevancies have been carefully eliminated and the relevant testimony has been strictly evaluated and coherently marshalled. This is especially true if papers are to be read in class and criticized by the class as well as the teacher — a highly desirable training in criticism for the class and in defense of his position for the reader. The reader's fellow-students will be able to detect irrelevances, bad method, awkward style, and pedantry better than inadequacy of information, but the former faults are, certainly at this stage of training, no less important than the last, and the teacher should be able to provide criticism of the last as well. If the subjects are so varied as to exceed one teacher's competence to control, he ought to call on his colleagues for assistance.

Bibliographical Aids and Expert Advice

The student should carry around in his head the kind of bibliography suggested above (pp. 72–3), and the instructor ought to help him to do so by requiring him to make one in writing. In addition the student ought to develop a few other reference habits. One of these is to call upon the staff of his library; they are trained to trace obscure bibliographical items and to find answers to little questions in less time than he can, though if he is familiar with Mudge's *Guide to Reference Books* (the so-called "reference librarian's Bible"), he will be able often to shift for himself. He should also be obliged to use whatever union catalogues (i.e., combined catalogues of more than one library) may be available in his vicinity. This would include the use of such bound volumes as C. F. Ulrich's *Periodical directory, a classified guide to a selected list of current periodicals foreign and domestic* (5th ed., New York, 1947) and the *Union List of Serials in the United States and Canada* (ed. G. E. Malikoff, 2nd ed.; New York, 1945), which indicates the runs of periodicals in American libraries and thus makes it possible to know what issues other libraries may own of any newspaper or magazine. The student should also be taught to consult by mail or interview any experts who may be able to give him information or any collectors who may provide him with materials. Government agencies, astronomical observatories, public and community libraries, museums, archives, and semi-public institutions usually expect to render that kind of service, and private collectors are proverbially cooperative. The exchange librarian of his own library is another useful agent for the historian to know; this librarian can help him to locate and to borrow by mail or to have microfilmed needed sources available in other libraries.

The Hypothetical Historical Review

The teacher of historical method would do well to pretend and have his students pretend that he is the editor of a historical review who has asked each member of the class to submit an article on an agreed subject. The hypothetical editor and the hypothetical contributor are thus more or less morally committed to each other. An editor of a learned review is seldom so fortunate as the teacher who merely grades students' papers without making suggestions for their improvement. The editor, feeling under obligation both to accept a requested contribution and to maintain the highest standards in his columns, generally reads, copy-edits, and amends the submitted versions (more than once if necessary) until a version is reached that is as good as the editor and the author in collaboration can make it. If the teacher will do likewise for papers submitted to his hypothetical review, the student will learn much about how to prepare an article for a genuine periodical, and hence a chapter of a book. Correcting and proofreading a manuscript, footnote structure, and other technical details of manuscript preparation, as well as the finer points of historical method, reasoning, and composition, can be effectively taught in this fashion. To be most effective, a hypothetical editor ought to have few hypothetical contributors.

The hypothetical editor ought to learn the preferences of some leading historical review as to manuscript typing, footnote style, proof marks, orthography, capitalization, punctuation, etc., so as to teach his class consistency in at least one preferred style. It might also be useful if the teacher would demonstrate from actual proofs of a galley and a page the problems that arise at those stages of publication. A discussion of the preparation of an index might not only serve to elucidate the complications involved in that trying process but might suggest to the hypothetical author some ways of using an index for historical research and examination preparation as well. Two books that will be helpful in preparing the hypothetical editor for his role are a *Manual of Style . . . recommended by the University of Chicago Press* (11th ed., Chicago, 1949) and John Benbow, *Manuscript and Proof* (3rd ed., New York, 1943).

Some Aids in Composition

The literature on style and composition is enormous. Good style can perhaps be acquired only by inspiration and perspiration, but, at least, a number of tools to work with have been provided. The teacher should insist upon their proper and frequent employment. Anyone who intends to make a serious occupation of writing would do well to own, in addition to a good dictionary, a thesaurus [1] (for syno-

---

[1] E.g., *Roget's International Thesaurus* (New York, 1946).

nyms), a dictionary of quotations [2] (for rhetorical bolstering of a point), a one-volume encyclopedia [3] (for ready reference), and a manual of correct English usage [4] (for guidance on debatable matters of grammar and style).

The Right Word and the Accurate Phrase

Since the difficulties of composition do not differ in historical writing from those of any other kind of composition, only a few that have special application to the historian need be mentioned here. Exactness of meaning is of special importance to the historian because he is attempting to convey the truth by the inadequate means of verbal expression. He is expected not only to create moods and to depict an atmosphere but also to present a complete and accurate account. The obligation to use words in their exact significance, to define his terms, to avoid synonyms that are only approximate rather than identical to what he means weighs more heavily upon him than upon the writer of belles-lettres. He is also under special obligation to avoid vague generalities and typifications as much as possible, if for no other reason than that the temptation to do so is especially attractive to him. Phrases like "the Athenian populace," "the middle class," "public opinion," "medieval man," "the Russians," etc. inevitably occur in his-

---

[2] E.g., H. L. Mencken, *New Dictionary of Quotations on Historical Principles* (New York, 1942); John Bartlett, *Familiar Quotations* (ed. Christopher Morley; 12th ed., Boston, 1948).

[3] E.g., *The Columbia Encyclopedia* (New York, 1944).

[4] E.g., H. W. Fowler, *A Dictionary of Modern English Usage* (Oxford, 1933).

torical writing, easily become personalized, lose their metaphorical character, and assume a concreteness out of all proportion to their real value as approximate averages, representative types, assumed majorities, or random samples. The frequent use of more accurate phrases like "a probable majority of the Athenian people" may be stylistically awkward, but if such a phrase is used at least the first time it is meant, perhaps thereafter — and particularly if the author himself continues to be aware of its fallacy — a shorter one like "the Athenians" may not be misleading.

Proper Identifications

The historian interested in his reader's reaction will avoid assuming too much knowledge on the part of the reader. Beginners in college classes frequently fail to bear this in mind because they are painfully aware that their reader is a probably well-informed professor. The professor, whether or not he poses as editor of a hypothetical learned review, can help them remember the average reader by pretending himself as he reads to have no more than a high-school education. As a rule, no proper name, such as of a person, place, official grouping, or event, should be introduced into one's writings without some kind of identification. Where the danger exists that such an identification will appear patronizing or pedantic, perhaps a mere title reminding the reader of the subject's position at the time of discourse will suffice — e.g., "Ex-president John Quincy Adams"; or an appropriate adjective might diminish the air of talking down to the reader by making it appear that the author takes for granted familiarity with the name being introduced — e.g., "the heroic Nathan Hale." In keeping with the same spirit, the given names of the persons in one's story should generally be used the first time he is introduced unless they are too hard to discover or unless, as frequently happens, he has so many given names (and the one he usually goes by is so hard to detect) that stating them all would verge on the ridiculous. In such cases, however, an adjective or a title frequently suffices — e.g., "one Mr. Jones," " Marquis de Lafayette." Exceptions can safely be made of names that are famous enough to be found in the average high-school textbook of history.

Editing a Document

Another stylistic weakness that the young historian should be especially warned against is over-long or over-frequent quotation. Documents become so important to the neophyte — and justifiably so — that he is likely to try to tell his story largely by means of quotations from them. He should be early informed that the place for the presentation of documents as such is in that section of learned reviews labeled "Documents." The teacher as editor of a hypothetical review might be well-advised to arrange with some of his hypothetical contributors to prepare such "Documents," especially if any unpublished materials worthy of the effort can be found. The "Documents" section of some historical periodical ought to be used as a model. Such articles should contain, in addition to the document itself, at least an introduction, giving the document its proper historical setting and explaining why it is regarded as important and authentic (or inauthentic), and a set of footnotes identifying proper names and obscure passages.

The Use of Quotations in Historical Writing

In historical narrative or exposition it is the historian's re-interpretation of what the documents teach that ought to be the prime objective. A document should be quoted, as a rule, only when the exact original wording is desirable or when it adds picturesqueness or rhetorical effect to the author's words. The reader's interest will lag if lengthy quotations are regularly introduced. They are so much unprocessed raw material, and it is usually better to refine them. This can be done easily, if more polished devices do not suggest themselves, by the author's paraphrasing of sentences within the body of the quotation.

Avoiding Artificiality of Style

The beginner is likely to assume that artificial rhetorical devices help to improve one's style. The historical present tense ("Pickett's division bravely defies the enemy's appalling fire and presses on across the field") is sometimes assumed to be more colorful than the past tense, as, indeed, it often is in colloquial narrative ("He says nothing, but ups with his fists and hits me in the eye"). It is doubtful, however, if frequent recourse to it in a historical narrative adds much more than affectation. The same holds true for all but the simplest similes and metaphors. Complicated figures of speech present in addition the dangers of the *cliché* and the mixed metaphor. The historian is especially tempted to speak in analogies to phenomena in natural history — birth, death, phylogeny, etc. — but the temptation should be resisted; it may complicate rather than simplify thought and in addition it may very well be of debatable accuracy. The use of foreign words and phrases is often also an affectation; even proper titles and names — as of companies, commissions, committees, etc. — should, wherever reasonable, be translated. And translations should not be awkward, unless the original was awkward; good idiomatic French, German, or Italian is well translated only in good idiomatic English — if necessary, by departure from literal translation.

Phrases That Reveal the Mental Machinery

Finally the teacher (or the hypothetical editor) should be on guard against "the smell of the lamp." Historians' writings are especially prone to this offense because of their anxiety to tell what they intend to do, to summarize what they have done, and to state no more than their evidence permits. Hence the frequent use of phrases like "I propose to show that," "it remains to demonstrate that," "it is safe to conclude that," "an analysis of the literature of the subject seems to warrant the statement that," "there is reason to believe that." The teacher of historical composition should stress that the process of deciding what is safe, warranted, or reasonable to set forth in a historical essay should have been carried on in the historian's head before he put pen to paper. What the reader wants and is entitled to have is the safe conclusion, the warranted statement, the reasonable belief; he expects the author's mental processes not to show. If "an analysis of the evidence justifies the statement that Kaiser Wilhelm II hoped to win a diplomatic victory without war in July, 1914," it is sufficient to state simply, "Kaiser Wilhelm II hoped to win a diplomatic victory without war in July, 1914." If necessary, references may be given in the footnotes to show why the simple statement is justified. It is obviously more difficult to avoid showing one's cerebrations when a negative result has to be indicated; for if there is little or no evidence to show that a point can correctly be made, it is the paucity or absence of the evidence that becomes the important fact to be stated. The very lack of evidence will not permit a simple, unqualified statement that something did not happen.

How Many Drafts of a Composition?

Before he gets ready to write, a historian ought to plan his article or chapter so as to have some idea what its beginning, middle, and end will be. Even when he does so, however, he generally has to compose with notes, books, newspapers, articles, photostats, microfilms, and other sources of information close at hand, since accuracy is one of his major objectives. The danger that the first draft will therefore sound like a lifeless juxtaposition of notes should be frankly admitted, although every effort to achieve literary polish should be made from the very beginning.

It sometimes happens that the first draft leads only to a realization that the whole composition has been wrongly conceived. This becomes especially apparent when the conclusion does not in fact follow straight and clear from the material that has been presented. In that case, it is best to start all over again, and, with the separate parts of the conclusion in mind, to prove each part step by step in a new composition.

After the first draft is finished, re-examination should be undertaken with a view to inserting any apparently relevant information that may previously have escaped attention. At this stage, if it has not been done already, it is wise to set down some brief indication of footnotes. These steps will probably leave a manuscript legible only to the author and, if he is lucky, his typist. Hence he ought to have a fresh draft made before it becomes totally illegible.

This second draft will probably have at most only one virtue — that of completeness. It will very likely lack smoothness of style, skillful transitions, and good organization, and, still more likely, it will have ir-relevancies, repetitions, and excess verbiage. The au-thor must now polish sentences and paragraphs, take the strain out of his transitions, remove irrelevancies and repetitions, transfer passages from places where they do not fit well to others where they fit better, and ruthlessly suppress unnecessary words, inadvisable superlatives, clichés, and mixed or far-fetched meta-phors. He must also take care to define his terms, identify obscure names and references, reduce the number and length of his quotations, smooth out his translations, and insert his footnotes in full. Perhaps, too, he should now re-examine his title, to see whether it fits what he has in fact written, and to devise a new one that will relieve him of the possible charge that his title promises more than he actually delivers. By this time the author has again made his typescript fairly illegible, and it should again be placed in the typist's hands for rewriting.

The third draft ought to be about as good as the author can make it. Nevertheless — and especially if some time has elapsed between drafts and he comes to the last as something new and strange — he will probably find many awkward or obscure passages that he will wish to change; and possibly also some things that seemed highly relevant in the second draft will appear less so on a fresh reading. These should now be revised — if necessary, at the expense of providing a fourth draft, at least of the affected pages. The longer the interval between drafts, the fresher the critical attitude the author will bring to each successive draft.

Polishing the Final Draft

A manuscript that is absolutely clean is suspect. A neat manuscript would not be one on which no corrections appear but rather one that shows signs of having been carefully and intelligently proofread and revised by the author. He should, however, take the pains to make his corrections easy for editors and printers (or, in a classroom, the teacher) to understand. An editor cannot be expected to piece together numerous inserts in the margins, between the lines, on separately attached slips, or on the reverse sides of pages. Where such insertions are lengthy or frequent, the offending page should be retyped.

Much bad writing of historical papers and dissertations results from (a) too brief intervals between drafts and (b) too few drafts. We may not all be able to put fire into our writing but we can all put our writing into the fire until a version worthy of a better fate appears. It is the business of the hypothetical editor to see that more than one draft is prepared, unless the paper, when first submitted, is so satisfactory as to indicate either exceptional talent or exceptional attention to the details of composition. Good historianship may be the result of qualities rarely found in combination, but indifferent historianship is frequently due to mere unwillingness to take pains with little things. And yet:

> Though little things perfection make,
> Perfection is no little thing.

PART THREE

Theory of History

CHAPTER IX

THE PROBLEMS OF SELECTION, ARRANGEMENT, AND EMPHASIS

HISTORICAL method is scientific if by *scientific* is meant "capable of ascertaining demonstrable fact" and if by *fact* is meant a detail derived from a critical examination of historical documents rather than a detail of past actuality. Fortunately or unfortunately, unconnected facts do not by themselves constitute the end-product of history. A description of past societies, conditions, ideas, and institutions or a narrative of past careers and events is usually the goal of the individual historical investigation. Such a description or narrative is frequently designated separately as *a history*; and, as previously stated, in their entirety the writings of history, or histories, are sometimes called *historiography*.

Historiography Redefined

New meanings attached to words already employed in other senses account for some of the confusion that arises in discussions of the nature of history. It may be well to repeat therefore that *a history* is a deliberate effort to give an account of some past event or combination of events; it is what is sometimes referred to as *written history*, as distinguished from *history-as-actuality* (or the total past of mankind whether known or not) and from *recorded history* (or that part of history-as-actuality which has somehow been placed on discoverable record, whether discovered yet or not). In an age in which lectures are not generally read from manuscript, as they were in the time before printing, *historiography* must also be interpreted to include *spoken history*, since the lecture, though a cheaper, more restricted, and less enduring means of publication than printing, is publication nevertheless. And *historiography* when meant to designate writings or literature that may be called historical has to be distinguished from the same word when meant to designate the process of writing history (i.e., putting together into a history the particulars extracted from the records by the careful application of the historical method). It is with historiography in the latter sense that the following pages deal.

Theories of Historical Synthesis

What historians all together as a group have striven to do has been to give as complete an account as possible of the past of mankind. The purpose of *historiography* at its highest (and quite unobtainable) level would be to re-create the totality of historical fact in a manner which does no violence to the actual past. In that sense, if it were possible, *historiography* might also be *scientific*, i.e., intended to discover and report the truth. As we have seen, however, the actual past can never be fully recovered in the mind. The experts differ even as to how it can be approximated. There are some who believe that an *objective* approach is possible; [1] there are others who maintain that historiography is an *art*, informed

---

[1] C. W. McIlwain, "The Historian's Part in a Changing World,"

by subjective philosophies, skills, learning, and memory;[2] there are still others who think that good guesses as to the major *trend* of history lay the bases for the best ordering of the facts.[3] It is possible that they are all partly right.[4]

*   *   *

Obviously the problem of writing history is not simple. In any kind of exposition or narrative, historical facts have to be (1) selected, (2) arranged, (3) emphasized or minimized, and (4) placed in some sort of causal sequence. Each of these processes presents its own set of complications.

The Problem of Relevance

The simplest rule of selection, it might appear, would be to choose that which is relevant. That, however, only shifts the difficulty to a decision of what is relevant. One way that is frequently suggested to keep the question of relevance in the forefront of one's mind is to think of one's subject always as a sentence rather than as a topic. Obviously, any historical topic can be stated in the form of a narrative, descriptive, or causal proposition. Thus "Conscription during the Second World War" becomes

---

American Historical Review, XLII (1937), 207–24; Louis Halphen, *Introduction à l'Histoire* (Paris, 1946).

[2] Carl Becker, "Everyman His Own Historian," *American Historical Review*, XXXVII (1932), 221–36; R. G. Collingwood, *Idea of History* (Oxford, 1946).

[3] C. A. Beard, "Written History as an Act of Faith," *American Historical Review*, XXXXIX (1934), 219–31.

[4] Cf. above pp. 8–25; Louis Gottschalk, "Scope and Subject Matter of History," *University [of Kansas City] Review*, VIII (1941), 75–83.

"During the course of the Second World War, nations X and Y resorted to conscription in raising their
armies." Such a proposition may prove true or false
upon investigation. If one assumes tentatively that it
is true, one accepts it as a hypothesis, or working
assumption. Similarly, if one assumes it is false. Unity
can be attained if one selects other propositions that
may help to establish the truth or falsity of one's
hypothesis, modifies it as the selected propositions require, and eventually becomes committed to a thesis
or to a suspension of judgment. This process of converting topic into proposition, proposition into hypothesis, and hypothesis into thesis clarifies the problem of relevance by breaking it into component parts,
indicating what must be relevant to what, and provides a means of discovering the unifying theme or
themes of a historical discourse. It does not entirely
solve the problem, however, since, reduced to its simplest terms, it says only that that is relevant which is
relevant to a unifying narrative, descriptive, or causal
proposition.

The Subject as a Question

The historian usually tries to solve the problem of
relevance in some such way (though all too often
without full awareness of the separate steps involved).
Usually the process can be simplified by converting
propositions into queries. As has been shown above
(pp. 141–3), the subject of any historical investigation may be expressed in the form of an interrogative
hypothesis. Thus, if we continue with the example
used above, the tentative topic "Conscription during

the Second World War" might become the interrogative hypothesis: "To what an extent was conscription employed during the Second World War?" This is obviously not the only question that the topic might suggest. The form the question might take would be determined by the interests of the questioner. He might prefer to ask: "What countries used conscription?" or "How many persons were conscripted?" or "How did conscription work?" But if his interests are not yet well formulated, some more general phrasing, such as "To what an extent?" would be preferable since it includes the others and is noncommittal. Further precision and limitation of interests and therefore of queries should not be too long delayed, however, lest time be lost in gathering materials that fit well under the more general question but would be irrelevant under the more precise one. The investigator now seeks for particulars that will enable him to answer his interrogative, ruthlessly eliminating those that do not lead to an answer or a suspension of judgment. The same objection, however, holds for this method as a complete solution of the problem of relevance as for the method that employs the unifying proposition. In the end, it says only that those things are relevant which are relevant to the answer to an interrogation.

The Four Aspects as a Standard of Relevance

By the time the historian reaches the writing stage of his investigation, the unifying proposition or the interrogative hypothesis should have become a full-fledged declarative thesis; otherwise he should suspend writing, unless he means only to explain why he can reach no conclusion. As a declarative historical statement, a thesis, even more precisely than a topic, involves four aspects — biographical, geographical, chronological, and functional. It has been pointed out (p. 53) that by a list of names, dates, and other keywords associated with each of these aspects, selections might be made in the taking of notes and thus the problem of relevance somewhat simplified. For the topic "Conscription during the Second World War" a set of keywords easily suggest themselves under each of the four aspects. Under the heading of biography would come persons or groups of persons — such names as "General Hershey," "draft boards," "conscripts," etc. Under the heading of geography would be included the names of countries in which conscription was contemplated or employed. Under the heading of chronology would come the period of conscription legislation. And under the heading of functions or occupations would come "legislation on conscription," "methods of conscription," "professions (e.g., military, naval, medical, legal) involved in conscription." By the time the investigation of this topic leads to a commitment on a thesis — let's say, "The system of military conscription alone could have provided the armies necessary for the defeat of Germany in the Second World War" — these categories should have become more clearly defined. By eliminating from each category keywords that are not related somehow to each of the other three, a fairly strict standard of relevance can be maintained.

Limited Helpfulness of the Proposition or Interrogative as a Subject

Both the unifying proposition and the interrogative hypothesis can be useful only for subjects so monographic in nature that their themes can be contained in a single proposition or interrogation (or causally connected group of propositions and interrogations). By definition, that rules out all subjects that have no narrative, descriptive, or causal synthesis but are held together only by association in time, place, or persons or only by analogy. Studies of that kind may not have a causal or organic unity, but the problem of relevance still adheres to them — perhaps *à fortiori*. Such subjects would include the history of a given region at a given time, of a collectivity of leaders of parties or movements, of schools of art and thought, and of analogous movements and institutions. For synthetic subjects like these, analysis by aspect keywords nevertheless can be useful if each of the separate elements in the synthesis is regarded as a separate monograph whose theme can be stated as a proposition or an interrogative hypothesis.

Despite the helpfulness of the unifying proposition and the interrogative hypothesis, the decision of what is relevant is largely a matter of personal judgment. Except in cases of blatant irrelevance or omission, the individual historian must be left to make his own selection of his data. One rule is certain: if a historical datum is relevant, it may not be disregarded, although after adequate consideration, it may properly be omitted from the final composition as unimportant. The lawyer's readiness to call adverse testimony "irrelevant and immaterial" should serve as a warning to the historian that he must always be prepared to establish that his data are neither.

Misuse of Footnotes to Solve the Problem of Relevance

In the effort to avoid strict judgments on the relevance of one's materials, a practice has become common that nevertheless seems to be unfortunate. That is to place data of doubtful relevance in footnotes. This practice gives an unnecessary air of pedantry to one's work and· is largely responsible for bringing the footnote into disrepute. Furthermore, it is a weak and slovenly way of solving the problem of relevance, for usually if the data are relevant they belong more properly in the text and if they are irrelevant they should be omitted entirely. The proper use of footnotes has already been indicated (pp. 19–21).

Helpfulness of Proposition or Interrogative as the Theme of a Monographic Study

In any event, to think of one's subject as a proposition the truth or falsity of which is to be established or as a question to which a correct answer is being sought would make the purpose of one's research stand out more clearly than it might when thought of as a topic. When historical subjects are thought of as topics, they do not discourage, and they may even encourage, the inclusion of anything that may be regarded as shedding light upon that topic. That is why books of history often go widely afield and sometimes contain long discussions of minutiæ whose connection with the discussion is so doubtful that they are dragged in by painfully obvious sentences (or even paragraphs) of transition, if they are not relegated to the footnotes.

If a historian has failed to understand the proper limitations of his inquiry, he might soon find that he has put hard work into learning many particulars that do not fit neatly into his composition. Still, believing, as historians frequently do, that all facts are created equal and are endowed by their discoverer with an inalienable right to citation, he might try to work them in somehow. If he were trying to establish the truth or falsity of a proposition or the answer to a direct question instead of aiming at as broad a target as possible, he would perhaps avoid some of the worst irrelevancies. And if he asked questions that had some relation to those that have constantly troubled mankind or if he merely kept such eternal questions in mind when asking ephemeral ones, he might perhaps avoid some of the worst trivialities. He would then agree with Lord Acton's dictum: "History compels us to fasten on abiding issues and rescues us from the temporary and the transient." [5] These admonitions would not apply, of course, with equal force where the historian's intention is to write a widely inclusive description of a place, period, movement, or career.

[5] "Inaugural Lecture on the Study of History," *Essays on Freedom and Power*, ed. Gertrude Himmelfarb (Glencoe, Ill., 1948), p. 5.

The Problem of Arrangement: Periodization

The most obvious arrangement of historical data is chronological, i.e., by periods of time. For *chronology* is about the only objective and constant norm the historian has to reckon with. Even chronology is only relatively objective, because *periodization* can be and often is arbitrary. Probably in no regard is this arbitrariness more conspicuous than in periodizing the history of ideas or movements. Catch phrases like the *Age of Faith*, the *baroque period*, the *Enlightenment*, the *Industrial Revolution*, the *Age of Metternich*, the *Century of Progress* sometimes lead to enough misrepresentation to outweigh their expected didactical advantage. They too easily give the impression that the distinguishing development or ideal did not exist at other times in striking proportions or that the ages so distinguished could not be correctly designated by some other name with equal accuracy. Assigning a descriptive term to a period of history may be a good way to give to that period a "frame of reference" in relation to which its values may be well understood, but that possible advantage is counterbalanced if it discourages a quest for other frames of reference. No age can be correctly described by a single, exclusive characteristic. Attempts to do so frequently result in ambiguous and metaphorical use of the characterizing term.

Great harm has, in fact, been done to the study of history by this tendency to attach only relatively appropriate labels to certain periods — notably in the division of history into *ancient, medieval,* and *modern.*

n the first place, ambiguous as these appellations are
even for western history, they fit other cultures still
ess; even where other cultures like the Chinese or the
apanese have gone through phases of development
hat seem to suggest an analogous transition from a
classical age through an intervening period to a modern era, the chronological limitations of these phases
do not correspond even roughly to the western ana-
ogues. In the second place, words like *ancient* and
medieval tend toward a prejudgment of remoteness,
deadness, and obsoleteness that would often be belied
f further examination were not thereby discouraged.
"The largest part of that history which we commonly
call ancient," said Dr. Thomas Arnold of Rugby, "is
practically modern, as it describes society in a stage
analogous to that in which it now is, while on the
other hand most of what is called modern history is
practically ancient, as it relates to a state of things that
has passed away." [6]

Current events loom large and take up many pages
n our history textbooks — more perhaps than are
given to Periclean Athens or Augustan Rome or the
Renaissance Italy; yet a generation hence they may
seem trivial. What historian now thinks the causes of
the First World War so important as most thought
they were in the generation between 1919 and 1929?
Historical perspective — that is to say, the ability to
see the proper role of a set of events in the long career
of mankind — comes only with the passage of time.
For that reason, it would be desirable if more (but by

[6] Vol. I, Appendix I, p. 636, of his translation of Thucydides
Oxford, 1820–35); cf. Thayer, I, 181.

no means all) historians were to devote themselves
to studying the enduring problems and the controlling
institutions or ideas in history — from their earliest
records to the present — rather than fixed periods of
history. That a tendency in that direction already exists is evinced by the increasing attention of historians
to phases of historical development such as economic
history, the history of culture, business history, agricultural history, etc.

Arrangement by Other Criteria

Other methods of arrangement than the chronological are possible but are likewise deficient. Geography may be an objective norm of arrangement, but
it is not constant (since in the course of time bound-
aries vary; rivers change their beds or dry up; volca-
noes become extinct; harbors are improved, canals
dug, waters damned, soils and mines exhausted by
man's efforts; flora and fauna migrate; climates are
defied; etc.). Yet an arrangement by *localities* may
sometimes be desirable. In dealing with problems of
personality, arrangement by *persons* or *groups of persons* (such as parties or nations) may seem best. In
dealing with social, economic, or other functions or
in endeavoring to answer questions previously posed,
arrangement by *problems* or *institutions* may be convenient.

It is appropriate to reiterate here a point already
made. In general, whatever arrangement other than
the chronological is used, it is good practice to adopt
at least a loose chronological form within each subdivision. Adherence to chronology may avert the ne-

cessity of repeating the narrative of the same events under different headings. Moreover, whatever *cause* may be (see below pp. 209–27), it usually is antecedent, though occasionally concurrent, in time to effect, and a strict chronological ordering is more likely to reveal and clarify it than a disregard of the progression of events.

The Problem of Emphasis: Space

The problem of emphasis is directly connected with the problems of selection and arrangement. An investigator, unless he leans over backward, runs the double risk of collecting more details on the points he believes important, if they are available, than on the points he believes unimportant, and of using that kind of arrangement which will give the important ones the most prominence. Besides, no matter how non-committal he may have been in the selection and arrangement of his data, he must make some decision regarding their relative importance when he begins to write, in order to determine the amount of space he will assign to each and the tenor of the language with which he will treat each. He can, of course, distribute space and emphasis according to the number of notes accumulated *per* particular. But such a quantitative distribution would often lead to greater attention to concrete trivia than to intangible though major phenomena. Generally more evidence is available on the banquets attendant upon international conferences, for example, than on the secret negotiations; and though it is easy to pile up minutiæ about many business operations, the motives of the persons

involved will frequently defy detection. Hence, the
historian can hardly avoid committing himself to a
thesis, and either stressing or minimizing his particulars in accordance with his evaluation of their importance in that thesis. Such an evaluation, like the
estimate of relevance, has to be left largely to personal judgment; though extremes of bad judgment
may often be detected and uniformly condemned by
his readers, even in the sounder instances a wide
margin of legitimate disagreement may nevertheless
arise among the experts as to the correctness of the
distribution of emphasis.

The Problem of Emphasis: Language

Difficult though the problem of space-distribution
may be in a historical essay, it is simple compared to
the subtleties of emphasis raised by the choice of
words. Two illustrations may suffice to point to the
pitfalls in word-selection.

(1) Suppose we choose two incontrovertible facts
about the same man: (a) Jean-Paul Marat was a
physicist, (b) he believed in terror as an instrument
of government in time of revolution. It is obvious
that those two facts can be put together in many ways,
none of which would be necessarily false, and yet each
of which would contain implications differing from
the others. E.g., "Marat, being a physicist, believed
in terror"; or "Though Marat was a physicist, he believed in terror"; or "While Marat was a physicist, he
believed in terror"; or "Marat was both a physicist
and a believer in terror"; or "Marat believed in terror
but was a physicist"; or "Marat was a physicist but

believed in terror"; and so on. Innocent and colorless words like *though, while, and,* and *but,* when they serve as conjunctions between facts, may assume a telling or misleading character.

(2) A story from the British campaign against Field Marshal Erwin Rommel in North Africa during the Second World War may illustrate another obstacle in the selection of the *mot juste.* Two British soldiers, tired and thirsty after hard fighting in the desert, return to their quarters and find half a bottle of water. "God be praised," says one, "it's half-full." "The Devil be damned!" exclaims the other, "It's half-empty." It is obvious that both were accurately describing a situation with regard to which each was a reliable eyewitness. Which of the two meaningful words, however, the historian of that situation (and similar situations) ought to use would depend neither on his training nor on his critical faculties but on a set of considerations in large part subjective.

The Desirability of Differing Interpretations

Musical compositions are more precise than written or spoken words, and musical instruments are a more mechanically accurate means for reproducing a composer's intention than is the human mind and hand or tongue for reproducing a witness's thought. And yet two equally talented virtuosi with the same score and the same instruments in hand, though they may agree on the scoring, may easily give differing interpretations to a piece of music, and perhaps it is desirable that they should. Musicians are, after a fashion, merely historians interpreting past achievements of a specialized nature. So are actors. If room for varying emphases and shadings exist in their interpretations, greater variety is inevitable among historians, who are obliged to express themselves in mere words.

Yet the same critic who might welcome two or more good interpretations of a Mozart sonata or of Hamlet may insist that there is only one correct interpretation of Mozart's or Shakespeare's life. That may be an indication, however, only that he has more flexible musical or histrionic standards than historical frames of reference. Can equally honest, competent, informed, and inspired historians disagree on their judgments of a phase of life as much as musicians on a musical interpretation without either of them being demonstrably wrong? The answer to that question requires an examination of the problems of cause and effect, of change and continuity in history.

CHAPTER X

THE PROBLEMS OF CAUSE, MOTIVE, AND INFLUENCE

Immediate Cause or Occasion

HISTORIANS tend to speak of the *immediate cause or occasion* and *remote or underlying causes* of historical events. The immediate cause of the First World War was the assassination at Sarajevo, and of the Second World War the Nazi invasion of Poland. The underlying causes in both instances included power politics, world anarchy, commercial rivalries, national aspirations, mutual fear, and territorial ambitions. On immediate causes it is relatively easy to secure agreement, though the difference of opinion among historians regarding the starting point of many a great movement indicates the possible range of disagreement even here. The Lutheran Revolt, for example, is variously said to have begun with the posting of the Ninety-Five Theses, the Disputation with Eck, the Diet of Worms, etc.; the American Revolution with the Stamp Tax, the Townshend Acts, the Boston Massacre, the Intolerable Acts, the Battle of Lexington and Concord, etc.; the French Revolution, with the Council of Notables, the calling of the Estates General, the formation of the National Assembly, the Tennis Court Oath, the Fall of the Bastille, etc.; the American Civil War with the election of 1860, Lin-

coln's decision to relieve Fort Sumter, the bombard-
ment of Fort Sumter, etc.

The "Occasion" as a Precipitating Accident

The immediate cause or occasion often seems to
partake of the nature of accident: if Henry VIII's
daughter Mary had been a son, Henry might not have
wished to divorce Catherine of Aragon and the English Reformation might not have come; if Louis XVI's
message had been properly delivered, there might have
been no Tennis Court Oath and hence no formal de-
fiance of the Old Regime of the Bourbons and no
French Revolution; or if Franz Ferdinand's chauffeur
had not taken a turn down a side street of Sarajevo,
the crown prince might not have become a good target
for assassination and the First World War might
have been averted.

But "the immediate cause" is not really a cause; it
is merely the point in a chain of events, trends, influences, and forces at which the effect begins to become
visible. It is the precipitating event that serves as the
dropping of a match in a combustible pile or the
tripping of a hammer on an explosive. As such it is a
good lead toward the antecedents that may be more
satisfactorily described as "causes." The more satisfying line of inquiry is not: What might have happened had this "accident" not occurred? It is rather:
How did circumstances get to such a pass? How could
a mere accident like the late delivery of a message or
the taking of a wrong turn in a parade lead to a world
revolution or a world war? When that line is followed,
the answer to "what might have been" usually be-

comes easy; one often becomes satisfied that, if not this accident now, some other later would have had the same effect, for the determining trends, influences, and factors were still operating. This is not always so, for the death of a great leader (a Cromwell, for example, or a Lincoln or a Lenin) sometimes seems to have made a great difference in the success of vital policies. But the death of a great leader, though it may be unexpected, is not a trivial accident. It is something different from the proverbial nail for the want of which a kingdom was lost. In general, if a kingdom can collapse because of a missing nail, the state of the kingdom and not the history of the nail should engage the historian's attention.

History Compared to the Natural Sciences

When historians discuss the problem of underlying causes, they disagree most often and most vehemently. For the causal explanations of events rest upon philosophies of history; and of philosophies of history, there is no end.[1] To be sure, in other sciences likewise experts disagree regarding fundamental interpretations. The function of certain bacteria or the distance of certain stars may be variously estimated from time to time, and with the new knowledge may come a radical

---

[1] Cf. Bernheim, pp. 1–43 and 685–749; Collingwood, *passim;* Robert Flint, *The Philosophy of History in France and Germany* (New York, 1874); F. J. Teggart, *Theory of History* (New Haven, 1925); Benedetto Croce, *History: its Theory and Practice* (New York, 1921); H. E. Barnes, *History of Historical Writing* (Norman, Oklahoma, 1937); G. L. Burr, "The Freedom of History," *American Historical Review,* XXII (1917), 253–71; J. W. Thompson, *History of Historical Writing* (New York, 1942).

reconstruction of the science of medicine or of astronomy. But the bacteria and the stars do not change because of a change in the observer and his fellow humans. It may be true, as Thomas A. Edison is supposed to have said, that we know only one-millionth of one percent of what there is to be known. But what the physicists lack in knowledge will have no effect upon the physical universe. The historian's world, however, now and potentially exists only in what is recorded directly or by inference therefrom. His knowledge of that world partly determines the nature of what is knowable by determining what parts of the record will receive special attention and thus be more certain of preservation. The changes in interpretation of the natural sciences are usually attributable to accumulation and correction of knowledge, rarely to the loss of data, and still less rarely to change in the object studied. In history they come quite often from the disappearance of sources and hence of part of the potentially knowable historical universe. At the same time, day by day, new history happens. Confronted by this partly diminishing, partly growing universe, which at best is only the record that symbolizes the unknowable "actual" universe of history, historians find it difficult to explain the "actual" historical universe by any generally acceptable concepts.

Causal Theories up to the Reformation

The Egyptian, Babylonian, and Greek historians for the most part thought of history as did Herodotus, who wrote his *History* in "the hope of thereby preserving from decay the remembrance of what men have done and of preventing the great and wonderful actions of the Greeks and barbarians from losing their due need of glory." [2] Hence they came to consider the prowess of great heroes, priests, and kings to be the principal cause of change in history. Developments that they could not explain in that way they were likely to attribute to the will of gods. Alongside of that philosophy — especially among the Greeks — ran the belief that history was a branch of didactic literature — for those, in Thucydides' words, "who desire an exact knowledge of the past as a key to the future." The Hebrews and the Romans subscribed to these ideas also, the former with special emphasis upon a single almighty God. All three peoples stressed the dramatic conflicts in history and thus came to think of the interplay of providence or fate and the unpredictable character of man as the chief moving force in history.

The Hebrew emphasis upon the direct intervention of God in the affairs of man led to a Christian belief in teleology, and Occidental historiography thus became in the Middle Ages the recording of the elaboration of man's worldly career according to a divine plan. With the split of the western Catholic world into two camps by the Reformation, Occidental history became largely a weapon of polemic among conflicting theological schools; again the emphasis shifted to human frailty and prowess as the best explanation of secular crises, though history remained essentially theological still.

---

[2] *The History of Herodotus,* tr. George Rawlinson (New York, 1909), 1, 27.

The Rationalists and the Causes of History

The development of deism and rationalism in the seventeenth and eighteenth centuries diminished the accent on God's plan and increased the interest in man's work and his place of abode. The supernatural, revelation, and divine inspiration as causal explanations of human developments yielded gradually to a new stress upon the natural and the regular. Hobbes, among others, believed man's nature to be competitive and his institutions to be derived from the necessity of keeping competition within endurable bounds. Locke, quoting "the judicious Hooker" [3] with approval, found on the contrary that "mutual love among men was the dominant characteristic of natural society and that their civil institutions are derived from reason and the desire to preserve their freedom, rights and privileges." Montesquieu stated that geographic environment molded and limited man's nature, institutions, and traditions; and the Physiocrats subscribed to a similar theory of a "natural order" for man's institutions. For many others among the French *philosophes*, man's perfectibility was the end toward which history tended unceasingly. Man's story on earth became a struggle between perfectible human nature and obscurantism (Voltaire's *infâme*); and in the prosecution of the war against the *infâme*, Voltaire wrote history, said Montesquieu, "to glorify his own convent, like any Benedictine monk." [4] Con-

---

[3] *Two treatises of government*, Bk. II, Ch. II.

[4] Quoted in Adolph Meyer, *Voltaire, Man of Justice* (New York, 1945), p. 312.

dorcet, one of the more historical-minded among the *philosophes*, set forth a theory of perfectibility through the steady accumulation of knowledge and the triumph of reason. The more materialistic of the eighteenth-century *philosophes* (like La Mettrie and Helvétius) thought of human nature as a compound of likes and dislikes, pains and pleasures. The romantic Rousseau considered it a compound resulting from the struggle of *amour-propre* and *pitié*, selfishness and altruism, vice and virtue.

Nineteenth-Century Philosophies

The nineteenth century, with its plethora of nationalisms, philosophic idealisms, utilitarianisms, and positivisms, showed even more varied approaches to the problem of cause than did any of the earlier periods. The idea of a fundamental character adapted to dominant physical circumstances and local situations (including traditions) had been earlier borrowed from Montesquieu by some German writers, conspicuous among whom was Herder, and was now broadened, notably by Savigny, into a persuasion that national characters existed which helped to mold the destiny of nations. In France, Michelet, leaning more heavily on Vico, an Italian contemporary of Montesquieu whom he had rediscovered, set forth much the same theory with regard to France. These men, by their emphasis upon national growth and institutions, gave to history, as opposed to nature, the chief place in the explanation of man's character and destiny.

Other schools of historical thought also flourished in the beginning of the nineteenth century. The reaction against eighteenth-century materialism gave a temporary victory to the Romantics, who again emphasized human emotions as the moving force in man's destiny. At the same time the idea of progress found its advocates in those who, like the Hegelians, the St. Simonians, and the Comteans, believed in a succession of cultures, each born out of the ashes of its predecessor. Hegel held that a new culture arose as representative of a new spirit (*Zeitgeist*) and took the place of an old culture that had ceased to be representative. St. Simon and Comte thought rather of societies succeeding each other because of increasing understanding of and control over nature and human affairs. Carlyle with his respect for the "hero" and his emphasis upon the idea of periodical decay and rebirth furnishes an excellent example of coexistence of the two ideas in one mind.[5] The concurrent development of the theory of biological evolution fortified also the belief in survival of the fittest (Darwin, Spencer).

The Marxian Interpretation of History

Meanwhile Malthus and his fellow economists had developed their theory of scarcity and hence of struggle for survival in the economic sphere. Karl Marx subsequently combined the Hegelian theory of succession of cultural patterns with the struggle for existence. The result was his explanation of change in history as materialistically determined: control of the modes of production determines which class and

---

[5] Cf. Hill Shine, *Carlyle and the St. Simonians, the Concept of Historical Periodicity* (Baltimore, 1941).

hence which patterns of thought would dominate at any given moment, but the continuous struggle among the classes must ultimately lead to the triumph of the proletariat.

Nationalism and Racism

For a long time the victory seemed to rest (and perhaps still rests) with the historians of the nationalistic schools. Since the "racism" of the Nazis has been so irrefragably exposed, few historians now speak of a "national character" as if it were something biologically inherited and are careful to limit the term "race" to groupings like the Caucasoid, the Negroid, and the Mongoloid, or to sub-groupings like the Mediterranean and the Alpine, to which anthropologists agree that the term belongs. Nevertheless, the persuasion that certain types of character belong to certain peoples in certain areas persists and gives rise to unfortunate stereotypes — "the Latin temperament," "Japanese cruelty," "Jewish shrewdness," "Gallican volatility," "German ruthlessness," "British phlegmatism." Much as these stereotypes are to be lamented if based upon unreflecting prejudice, they have a limited validity if they are intended to convey the idea that within certain cultures certain values have been inculcated by tradition, the ethnical institutions, and the system of formal education. Such a possibly justifiable concept of a national character, however, will err decidedly if it leaves no room for the large numbers in any state or society who fail to conform to type and for the instances when even the most conforming individual may act untypically. Nevertheless, since the time of Herder, there has developed a confidence in the *Volksgeist* (the national character) as a means of effecting change in history (Savigny, Michelet, Macaulay, Sybel, Treitschke, Bancroft, Maurras).

Today it is perhaps the dominant creed — though, in most instances, subconsciously — of most historians, rivaled only by those who, more consciously, advocate the Marxian philosophy. It has had the support of governments not so much by their direct encouragement of national historians as by the development since the French Revolution of national support of national archives, national libraries, national historical societies, and national historical periodicals — in all of which the major attention is generally given to the national history.

Scientific History

A reaction to the proliferation of philosophies of history also set in during the nineteenth century and continues to our own day. At first it led to the formation of a school of "scientific" historians, nearly all of them directly or indirectly the students of Ranke. They believed it was possible to tell how history "actually happened" without any philosophy of causation or with only *ad hoc* philosophies, each adapted to a particular historical sequence. They and their successors hold that the best philosophy of history is no all-embracing theory of causality but a concatenation of antecedents and consequents. They do not explain, however, how, from the infinity of things that go before and the infinity of things that follow after any historical event, one knows which are antecedent and which consequent in the logical as well as chronological order. Though they still are doing valiant service in testing, compiling, and editing source collections (thus continuing a tradition of erudition begun in the seventeenth century), their writings achieve no greater scientific objectivity than those of their predecessors. Ranke himself, though earlier he had adopted a sort of humanitarian world-view of history, in his later life developed a theory of history that appeared to be based upon a concept of conflict among nations for power.

The Historical School: Historicism

Toward the end of the nineteenth century, especially in Germany, "the historical school," or "historicism," as it is sometimes called, became prominent. This movement, too, was partly a reaction to the rational abstractions of the Enlightenment. Enlightenment rationalists had maintained with Descartes and Rousseau that reason was superior to history as a source of knowledge and that where a logical abstraction conflicted with historical experience, so much the worse for history, which might be only the story of the illogical results obtained by the application of mistaken philosophical principles. The Abbé Sieyès, who probably wrote more constitutions than any other one man in history, refused to write his memoirs because he believed that each generation must learn from its own experience; and perhaps that explains what was wrong with his constitutions.[6]

---

[6] C.-A. Sainte-Beuve, *Causeries du lundi* (Paris, 1852), V, 173-4.

In contrast to that rationalist point of view, the historicists claimed with Hegel that a universal history was in continual process and that empirical historical inquiries, if properly fitted into the universal process, could help to elucidate its development. They shared also Ranke's opinion that fact could be distinguished from falsity by a strict application of the historical method, but parted company from those Rankeans who felt that historical inquiry should be divorced from philosophical interpretation. Among the philosophical principles that they especially emphasized was that history should be a quest for values, providing "explanation and guidance for the life of the present day." [7] The human mind was for them not a product of Nature but of History and its operations could best be understood by an application of the historical spirit to contemporary sociological problems. Wilhelm Dilthey, one of the leading historicists, developed along these lines a sort of socio-psychological school of history and, more particularly, of biography.

American Interpretations of History

Ranke's leading American disciple was Herbert B. Adams, who introduced the Rankean seminar method of training historians into Johns Hopkins University. Thence it spread to American universities generally. Adams appears to have believed in an Anglo-Saxon racial character from which American historical devel-

---

[7] Wilhelm Dilthey, *Einleitung in die Geisteswissenschaften* in *Gesammelte Schriften*, I (Leipzig, 1922), p. xvi. See also pp. 110–11 above.

opment was largely derived. Frederick J. Turner, one of Adams's students, differed with Adams chiefly regarding the dominant source of the American character, insisting that the influence of the frontier and a resulting sectionalism were more important than the European inheritance. Recent historians of immigration and its effects upon American culture, several of them students of Turner, re-emphasize the European roots but spread them more widely through the European soil. Separate from this line of descent is Captain A. T. Mahan who has turned the historian's attention to sea power as an influence in the determination of the destiny of nations. The United States has had, along with these schools, its theological, nationalist, Marxian, geographic-determinist, "scientific," and other schools of historians as well.[8]

The Pluralistic School of Historical Causation

Another school of historians to react against the clamor of nineteenth-century philosophers, each claiming to have found the single correct explanation of historical change, may be called the "pluralists." Since Voltaire's day at least there has been, in reaction against the kind of history that merely chronicles gala events and the deeds of prominent men, a growing insistence upon a "new history" that will deal with social, cultural, political, and economic developments — the varied pattern of mankind, the manifold development of civilization.[9] Implicit in this concept of the fullness of the human past is the assumption

---

[8] Randall and Haines, *loc. cit.*, pp. 5–52.

[9] Cf. J. H. Robinson, *The New History* (New York, 1912).

that there are several acceptable orderings of history rather than a single correct one. Historians today tend to make a pluralistic interpretation of cause.

Some striking monistic philosophies, to be sure, have been presented recently. Spengler [10] and Toynbee [11] employ morphological explanations of growth and decay; Sorokin adopts a Comtean epistemological interpretation (i.e., a succession of cultures varying according to their sources of higher knowledge) minus Comte's faith in indefinite progress.[12] It has been maintained that several contemporary philosophers of history — Spengler, Toynbee, Bergson, Pareto, Ortega y Gasset, Croce, etc. — contending that Reason carries with it the seed of destruction of the vital process of civilized life, and seeking for some faith not wholly sanctioned by Reason, believe in the rise, maturity, and decay of cultures that have no redeeming faith.[13] But within their all-embracing morphological philosophy they leave (Toynbee, in fact, insists upon) room for a series of lesser causes to operate.

A Recent Effort to Define Cause

Few writers still insist that man's fate is determined alone by his geographical and climatic environment,

---

[10] Oswald Spengler, *Decline of the West*, tr. C. B. Atkinson (New York, 1926–8).

[11] A. J. Toynbee, *A Study of History* (London, 1935–9).

[12] P. A. Sorokin, *Social and Cultural Dynamics* (New York, 1937–41).

[13] Rushton Coulborn, "Historian's Consolation in Philosophy," *Southern Review*, VII (1941), 40–51; Rushton Coulborn and W. E. B. Du Bois, "Mr. Sorokin's Systems," *Journal of Modern History*, XIV (1942), 500–21.

or by his search for bread, or by original sin. Recently a group of American historians, in a formal set of "Propositions" regarding the historical studies in the United States, announced in Proposition XI their acceptance of a pluralistic philosophy:

The term "cause," as used by historians, must . . . be regarded as a convenient figure of speech, describing motives, influences, forces, and other antecedent interrelations not fully understood. It may be defined as any preceding event in what is assumed to be a consequential and interrelated complex. It follows from this definition that a "cause" never operates except as part of a complex or series. Consequently the phrase "the cause" while justifiable when used to indicate a precipitating event or phenomenon, should be avoided in favor of its plural, "the causes," which likewise should be used only with great circumspection.[14]

This is a roundabout admission that the authors of this proposition are somewhat baffled by the problem of causation. Instead of defining what it is, they say it is an "assumed" complex of things "not fully understood" — "a convenient figure of speech" that "should be used only with great circumspection." In fact, the preceding Proposition (X) reveals their bafflement even more clearly:

The concept of causality has entered into narrative to such an extent that the writing of history might become mere cataloguing or chronology without it. Historians should be aware, however, that investigation of "cause" in history must be posited on two arbitrary limitations:

---

[14] Merle Curti *et al.*, p. 137.

(1) of the extent of past time in which antecedent inter-relations will be sought, and (2) of the number of im-pinging factors that will be assumed to remain constant and therefore will not be examined. In terms of these lim-itations the moot question of First or Single Cause is a metaphysical and not a historical problem.[15]

Two of the committee that drew up these propositions refused to subscribe to this one, stating that they felt "that the terms 'cause' and 'causality' should never be used in written-history." [16] For different reasons, those who contend that God's Will and those who contend that a Natural Order rule the universe might also ob-ject to the use of *cause* on the grounds that, every-thing being predetermined, it is either meaningless or self-evident.

The Desirability of Some Theory of Causation in History

It must be admitted that the problem of historical causation is still essentially unsolved; and in our pres-ent state of knowledge a judgment of philosophies of history as right or wrong, intelligent or unintelligent, adequate or inadequate, good or bad, grand or petty, must rest upon debatable criteria. Many historians still take the nihilist attitude regarding philosophies in history: they are all bad; let's have none of them. But danger lurks in such nihilism. It is a danger not merely of formlessness in what they write (since ni-hilism presents no criteria whatsoever for selection,

---

[15] Ibid., p. 136.
[16] Charles A. Beard and Alfred Vagts, ibid., pp. 136–7, n. 3.

arrangement, and emphasis) but also of meaningless-
ness (since data set down in purely chronological or
alphabetical order — about the only orders possible
without some philosophy — are likely to be mere statements of *what* without explanations of *why*, *how*, and
for what good or bad). But if such historians are at a
loss, part of the blame lies at the door of the social
scientists and philosophers. History as *Geschichtswissenschaft* (i.e., as a branch of knowledge dealing with
past events) does not devise general principles (except within the limits that will soon be described in
Chapter IX). It depends upon the *Gesetzwissenschaften* (i.e., branches of knowledge concerned with laying down generalizations) for its general principles
(cf. p. 251 below). Often the general principles of the
Gesetzwissenschaften are unsatisfactory, debatable,
or obscure, and thus have small effect outside the circles that debate them. That, however, does not excuse
the historian for indifference to them, for philosophical systems and sociological laws are a possible means
of discovering the causal relations among historical
phenomena.

Desirability of More Precise Words than "Cause"

The definition of cause as "a convenient figure of
speech" obviates some but not all the difficulties connected with it. Proposition XI, quoted above, by calling a cause "a preceding event" admittedly is dealing
only with that kind of cause which philosophers since
Aristotle have called "efficient cause," i.e., the antecedent producing agency without which the conse-

quent, known as "the effect," could not be.[17] But some causes need not be antecedent. Influences, for example, may be persistent (as of literature) and even reciprocal (as of one's family); means have to be concurrent if they are instruments by which the cause is effected, and even more so if they are the material out of which a product is made. Aristotle spoke not only of *efficient* causes but also of *formal, material,* and *final* causes. The efficient cause of building my house is the builder; its formal cause is the architect's design; its material cause is the conglomeration of things that went into its building; and its final cause is my purpose to have a house (and to pay for it). The problem remains complicated enough, even if one thinks of cause merely as efficient cause, and even if one agrees (in keeping with the conditions laid down in Proposition X) not to go constantly backward in time seeking the cause of the cause of the cause *ad infinitum,* and, in looking (let's say) for the causes of the Treaty of Versailles of 1919, not to inquire, into the physics of the Hall of Mirrors at Versailles and the biochemistry of the Big Four.

A fuller inquiry into cause would oblige one to answer not only the question "How?" but also the question "Why?" If *how* means *by what process and*

---

[17] The weaknesses in Propositions X and XI are at least as much my responsibility as that of any of my colleagues on the Committee on Historiography. In the present volume, I have profited from the private comments received by the Committee after its *Report* was published, and especially those of Professor E. W. Strong. See also his "Fact and Understanding in History," *Journal of Philosophy.* XLIV (1947), 617–25, and "How is Practice of History Tied to Theory," ibid., XLVI (1949), 637–44.

means, one is concerned with determinisms (social, natural, supernatural, and other), with accident, with historical trends, with biological, mechanical, and technological methods, etc. Even where these seem to involve historical developments, they have a philosophical component. If *why* means *for what purposes*, psychological factors — such as objectives, motives, drives, and personal influences — need to be considered. And psychology is no more adequate and satisfactory as an auxiliary to the historian than is philosophy. Perhaps historians ought to use the word *cause*, and even the word *causes*, sparingly and instead, breaking the concept down into its component parts, cultivate the more precise words — imprecise though they too may be — such as "purpose," "occasion," "antecedent," "means," or "motive," wherever possible. At any rate, constant awareness of the problem is desirable if it leads to strenuous efforts to use words having causal connotation only with special attention to precision.

The Problem of Motives

Schools of thought regarding human motivation are closely related to the schools of thought regarding historical causation. Those who believe in the economic determination of human conduct (which should be distinguished from the Marxian materialistic, or technological interpretation) must necessarily have a great confidence in man's consistent action for reasons of self-interest as well as a theory regarding where self-interest ends and altruism begins. Those who believe in predestination must believe in a driving force derived from inner grace. Those who believe in the subordination of the individual to the authority of the state often accept Hobbes's description of man as fundamentally competitive and belligerent. Those who believe in liberty often share Rousseau's confidence in man's altruism and his *faculté de se perfectionner*.

The belief now growing in favor among psychologists that each separate human act has its own history is appealing to historians. For generalizations are apt to prove inadequate when applied to particular individuals. "Men are in many respects alike. They have common needs for food, sex, activity, and society; common wishes for security, recognition, adventure, and response; but in their larger aspirations they differ because of particular historic traditions, particular environmental conditions, and the particular experiences of each personality." [18]

Man is a thing, an animal, and a human being. As a thing he has a physics and a chemistry. As an animal, he has an ancestry, an anatomy, a physiology, and a psychology. As a human being he has institutions, situations, traditions, and aspirations, and is subject to both inward and outward psychological urges and pressures. His conduct as a thing and an animal is largely divorced from rational considerations. As a human being his behavior may be either rational or irrational. In any event it is determined by physical, biochemical, genealogical, social, and psychological

---

[18] Quincy Wright, "The Universities and the World Order," *Bulletin of the American Association of University Professors*, XXXIII (1947), 50.

factors. It is physiological as well as sociological with a large admixture of mere inertia or kinetic energy. That is perhaps why no general theory of motivation has yet been propounded by students of personality (whether sociologists or psychologists) which entirely satisfies them or students of history.[19] The one most often cited is that of Thomas and Znaniecki, who set forth "the four wishes":

Every individual has a vast variety of wishes which can be satisfied only by his incorporation in a society. Among his general patterns of wishes we may enumerate: (1) the desire for new experience, for fresh stimulation; (2) the desire for recognition, including, for example, sexual response and general social appreciation, and secured by devices ranging from the display of ornament to the demonstration of worth through scientific attainment; (3) the desire for mastery, or the "will to power," exemplified by ownership, domestic tyranny, political despotism, based on the instinct of hate, but capable of being sublimated to laudable ambition; (4) the desire for security, based on the instinct of fear and exemplified negatively by the wretchedness of the individual in perpetual solitude or under social taboo.[20]

Few historians, however, are acquainted with the theoretical literature on human motivation.[21] There

---

[19] Cf. Allport, pp. 132–4, and E. M. Hume, *History and its Neighbors* (New York, 1942), p. 179.

[20] W. I. Thomas and Florian Znaniecki, *The Polish Peasant in Europe and America* (Boston, 1918–20), I, 72–3. Cf. R. E. Park, "The Sociological Methods of William Graham Sumner, and W. I. Thomas and Florian Znaniecki" in S. A. Rice (ed.), *Methods in Social Science, a Case Book* (Chicago, 1931), pp. 174–5.

[21] G. W. Allport, *Personality, a Psychological Interpretation* (New York, 1937) gives much attention to theories of human mo-

is a greater acquaintance (and perhaps misuse) of
Freudian psychoanalysis among them. But, discount-
ing the psychologists' and the social psychologists'
theories of personality (often without knowing them),
biographers usually build up *ad hoc* theories in keeping with the documentation of each individual case.
The psychologists have, however, made historians cautious regarding the validity of the conscious motive,
and aware of the differences between "good" reasons
and "real" reasons, between avowed purposes and
subconscious drives (though the historian must continue to expect that achievements may be the outcome of the "good" no less than the "real" reasons,
and of the avowed no less than the subconscious purposes). Biographers now commonly use (and perhaps abuse) the concept of *rationalization*.[22] Likewise,
the *unconscious, complexes, psychoses, frustration,
trauma, compensation, sublimation, transference, identification*, and similar psychological terms are gradually becoming familiar to them, and, it is hoped, will
become more familiar still.

Dominant Traits and Personality

Social psychologists are perhaps in part responsible
also for a recently renewed emphasis upon the significance of leadership and personality in social movements — a significance which even Marxist historians

tivation; see especially, pp. 55–97 and 190–231. See also W. A.
Weiskopf, "Cultural Conflicts and the Political Community,"
Common Cause, III (1949), p. 51 and n. 3.

[22] Cf. Franz Alexander, "Psychology and the Interpretation of
Historical Events" in Caroline Ware (ed.), *The Cultural Approach
to History* (New York, 1940), pp. 48–57.

now concede.[23] One of the most "sociological" of historians, while denying that the spontaneous aspirations of individuals can decide the course of events, since that course is predetermined by the conjunction of an infinity of antecedents, admits that human efforts sometimes help to shape events, although along with so many other factors as to have no appreciable effect in changing their inevitable outcome.[24] Some conventional historians may still find it hard to write nameless history (*histoire sans noms*), but they are becoming less and less averse to the history of classes, institutions, and movements in which individuals are subordinated. It ought not to be impossible to find the golden mean that exists somewhere between the *histoire sans noms* of some anthropologists and the *noms sans histoire* of some biographers.

The bearing of external factors upon personality has long been known to the biographer. Renan's *Jesus* illustrates that point, and it is implicit in Taine's theory of *race, moment, milieu* and *faculté maîtresse* as the determinants of historical developments. In recent years the importance of the milieu has been generally accepted by the more scholarly biographers, and biography has become largely an effort to place an individual in a social, political, cultural, or economic setting rather than to narrate a detached, personalized story. Nevertheless, the temptation is still great for the biographer through a kind of vicarious

[23] Cf. Louis Gottschalk, "Leon Trotsky and the Natural History of Revolutions," *American Journal of Sociology*, XLIV (1938), 339–54.

[24] Richard Bendix, "Max Weber's Interpretation of Conduct and History," *American Journal of Sociology*, LI (1946), 525.

egocentrism, to see his subject's times through his subject's eyes, making him too greatly the center of action and apologizing (or condemning) too much. It
is a temptation that can be counterbalanced by an
effort to remember that the social-cultural-personal
situation probably reacts upon personality at least as
often as it is affected by it.

Variability of Personality

The sophisticated historian needs but to look upon
his own development to perceive that a static portrait
of the personality or of the ideas of any historical
figure may be a good likeness for only a brief span of
his life. Personalities develop, ideas grow, and attitudes change. Yet biographers and students of the
history of ideas are all too prone to use such phrases
as "Caesar's ambition," "Frederick the Great's cyni-
cism," or "Gandhi's philosophy" as if they described
constants, or at least dominant and easily recogniz-
able things. Caution in specifying the particular period of life during which a trait was predominant —
perhaps even the particular occasion — is sometimes
all the more necessary when a phrase has come to represent a popular stereotype — such as the wisdom of
Plato, the cruelty of Messalina, the bravery of Richard
the Lion-hearted, the wickedness of the Borgias, the
inconsistency of Rousseau, the truthfulness of Washington, the democratic fervor of Lafayette, and the
ruthlessness of Bismarck. Even the greatest characters
and minds of the past have had to endure growing
pains; the historian disregards an essential part of his
task if he speaks of their personalities as if they were

invariable and always full-grown. That kind of error resembles the oversimplification that induces historians sometimes to write of a period of history or of a national group as if it had a single dominant aspect that makes attention to its other aspects unnecessary (see pp. 202–4 and 217 above).

Influence Defined

We have already mentioned "influence" (e.g., p. 221). It now needs to be defined more explicitly. As used here, it refers to "a persistent, shaping effect upon the thought and behavior of human beings, singly or collectively." By being "persistent" as well as an effect, it is distinguished from such single-occasion or passing factors as *instigation* or *enticement*; and by being "shaping" as well as an effect, it is distinguished from mere passive acceptance — as, for instance, of a fashionable school of thought or a momentary set of pressures. Because the word *influence* is loosely used, needless difficulty arises. Thus, if one is said to be "under the influence of alcohol," it is not clear whether he is temporarily drunk or a confirmed alcoholic. As the word "influence" is used here, the phrase would convey only the latter idea, and for the former we should prefer some wording like "under the temporary effects of alcohol." The difference is important to the historian because temporary effects may be more easily witnessed than the shaping effected by a persistent factor. Many historical studies try to estimate the influence of individuals, things, ideas, institutions, or episodes. Since the notion of *influence* is rather abstract and there is no generally accepted standard of measurement for it, such an effort is likely to lead to error, or at least to disagreement among the experts.

Posthumous Reputation Distinguished from Influence

The evil (and the good) that men do may or may not live after them. In any case, it is one thing to examine the *Nachruhm*, the posthumous reputation, of a personality or an event, and quite another to estimate its significance as a drive or impetus or shaping force in other personalities or events. *Nachruhm* may be myth (wholly fictitious) or legend (based upon a truthful fraction); it may even take the form of a cult, such as the Confucius cult in China, the Joan of Arc cult in France, the Lincoln cult in the United States, and the Lenin cult in Russia, or of a religion, such as Christianity and Mohammedanism, where obviously truth, myth, and legend have become inextricably interwoven, where symbol has often replaced actuality, and where dogma, creed, and tradition have squeezed out the recorded word.

But the *Nachruhm* of a historical figure is not necessarily correlated with or in itself a proof of his contemporary influence, though it may have a marked influence of its own. Christianity is based largely on the *Nachruhm* of Jesus, but it is historically more a result of Paul's influence than Jesus's; and if Trotsky had won over Stalin in Russia, the part of the Lenin credo that would now be most influential in Russia would be quite different from that which Stalin has chosen to make orthodox. *Nachruhm* may be the result of hothouse breeding, whether deliberate or unintentional. The Russians apparently have engaged for propaganda purposes in claiming a set of "firsts" by Russian scientists and inventors; it has been noted that English genius when measured by the number of inches of print needed to describe it in the *Encyclopædia Britannica* may shrink when measured by the *Grande Encyclopédie*.[25] It is an intriguing fact that at certain times and places in history men of outstanding ability and "influence" appear in "clusters." [26] It is possible, however, that these clusters may be the creation of the historians rather than of history — in other words, that the clusters may be only the outcome of a lively subsequent historical interest in certain kinds of activity. If we knew more about less well-remembered geniuses, these clusters might be less impressive.

Conspicuousness Distinguished from Influence

It is therefore obviously not sufficient to prove that a man, an idea, or an event was often recalled afterwards if one wishes to establish the extent of his or its contemporary influence. It is conceivable that a person or thing might be glorified contemporaneously or posthumously and yet have been uninfluential. Conversely, the flowers that were born to blush unseen might also have lent their unrecorded mite to the world's supply of honey.

Notwithstanding, at least one historian has maintained that the place to be given to a historical figure

---

[25] Sorokin, II, 141–4.

[26] Cf. A. L. Kroeber, *Configurations of Culture Growth* (Berkeley, Calif., 1944).

in a narrative is "proportionate to the relative importance that the different kinds of witnesses give
him." [27] This is almost equivalent to assuming that
conspicuousness is synonymous with *influence*. While
there is frequently a high correlation, however, between the two qualities, it is not a necessary correlation. There are "influences" which are totally unknown
to the historian; there are others that are great or little,
far out of proportion to their degree of conspicuousness; and there are still others that seem to grow or
diminish with the historian's attention to them. A
sensational crime or a best-selling novel will be given
"relative importance" by all kinds of witnesses. The
Piccini-Gluck controversy of 1777–8 got much more
attention than the contemporaneous experiments of
Lavoisier from high and low, wise men and fools; and
the Diamond Necklace Affair got more than the struggle for Huguenot toleration going on in 1785–7. On
the other hand, the village Hampdens, the mute in-
glorious Miltons, and the Cromwells guiltless of their
country's blood may be rescued from obscurity tomorrow, and then suddenly "the extent of their consequences" [28] will increase, perhaps by a re-assessment
of their significance for the past and, at any event,
for the future.

27 Halphen, p. 60.
28 Ibid., p. 59.

Measurement of Influence as a Subjective Process

The "objective importance" [29] of an unknown career or of a forgotten episode is itself unknowable. Historical importance has no existence except as an abstract that the historian can estimate only theoretically, and only for recorded personalities and events. In short, "influence" does not exist for him unless he discovers some record of it or of the influencing person or thing. Examples can be multiplied to illustrate that now admittedly significant developments were once lost to history and hence had no "objective importance" that the historian could even guess until they came into his ken, and that now neglected developments may eventually have greater "objective importance" than the present historian can possibly guess. Was Hammurabi's "actual" influence any less on legal institutions because historians before Rawlinson could not read his code? Was Ikhnaton's effect on the religious thought of intervening ages created only when Champollion deciphered hieroglyphics? Was Aristotle's influence as a political commentator made any greater on the centuries that had lost his *Constitution of Athens* because at the turn of our century it was rediscovered? If some Carthaginian historians had survived and received a fraction of the attention won by Roman historians, would there not be more Carthaginian references in our encyclopedias today, even though Carthaginian influence would be no greater? If recently many

[29] Ibid.

textbooks have taken to mentioning Emeric Crucé, an early advocate of collective action for peace, has his "objective" influence on intervening generations thereby increased? Was Pugachev "objectively" negligible merely because, until the Russian Revolution, he was neglected? If by some chance spiritualism should in the future be found to have some sort of scientific basis (as proved to be the case with Mesmerism), will not the "extent of the consequences" of some people who today look a little silly become quite enormous? If reputations rise or fall, if someone who was forgotten centuries or decades ago is famous today and someone who is famous today will be forgotten tomorrow, it is not because of any change in his "real" qualities or his "objective importance," but rather because of shifts in the historian's sources, attention, and knowledge.

Later Influence Not an Intrinsic Quality

The "influence" of an event or person on any subsequent generation may depend, at least part of the time, on the cultural pattern of the generation influenced rather than on the intrinsic quality of the past event or person. Ideas, for example, are seldom new. If a Locke, a Voltaire, or a Marx have great "influence," it may be attributable to their own articulateness or the acceptability of their writings, but it is also likely to be attributable to the greater degree of receptivity in their readers because of certain extrinsic circumstances. Consider the "influence" of Franklin D. Roosevelt or of Joseph Stalin or of U 235. What standards can there be other than events that have not yet happened to tell us whether the ideals of Roosevelt will be more "influential" in the long run than the ideals of Stalin or whether the now relatively obscure discoverers of U 235 will not render both equally uninfluential? We can, of course, make some effort to measure "the extent of their consequences" until today. But we would still have to recognize that our estimate of "influence" can be nothing more than a guess as to what might have happened, what might have been the shape of affairs, if the influencing force had not existed or acted as it did. That is a difficult process requiring an estimate of the rôle of every other possible factor and an elimination of the "influence" or, at least, a suspension of judgment upon it if it could logically be replaced by any other. We shall return to this problem shortly (pp. 242–3).

Relative Greatness or Degree of Influence

"Influence" is not a uniform thing. Sometimes various kinds of influence are incomparable and incommensurable. If one were to contend, for example, that Dr. Jenner, who invented the first dependable method of inoculation against smallpox, ought to be given more space in history textbooks than his contemporary, Napoleon Bonaparte, because the doctor was a "greater" (i.e., in this context, "more influential") man, one seems immediately to be confronted with an implied definition of *greatness*. It would appear from the preference for Jenner that such a definition of *greatness* comprised influence for good but not for evil; it would therefore be measured in this instance probably only by effect upon the decline of the death rate but not upon its increase. And yet who can tell whether the effect of Napoleon in one direction was less or more important than the effect of Jenner in the other? The problem is made somewhat more complicated by the fact that at intervals at least the birth rate actually appears to have risen in Napoleonic France.

And here we are dealing with commensurates (assuming that the necessary data for a comparison were available). When we come to estimate the significance of Napoleon's reforms or of his conquests, what norm can we use that would enable us to compare it with the significance of Jenner's discovery? Perhaps their effect too upon the birth rate. But that effect would be indirect and would require quite a complicated, speculative process to measure, even granted that the data were available.

Intellectual Influences

At least, if we talk in terms of comparative effect on birth and death rates, we know what we mean by *degree of influence* and *greatness* even when we cannot measure them. Napoleon and Jenner might conceivably be compared also in terms of their effect upon the national incomes of France and England, and thus would have some additional commensurable quality. But what can be done to clarify the concept of intellectual influence? Too often students of the history of ideas are content to establish a similarity between two sets of ideas, and to argue *post hoc, ergo proper hoc*. That is obviously insufficient. That Milton had ideas similar to Virgil's or Jefferson to Confucius's may be due to other factors than the direct shaping of the later man's ideas by the earlier man's. The influence may be at second or third hand, or many more stages removed; or both may have been influenced by an independent third person. The similarity may be due to a tradition so ancient and tenuous that its course may be more apparent than real. It may be due to a set of similar experiences to which both were exposed and to which both reacted similarly without any indebtedness of the later writer to his predecessor. It may be derived from the similarity between the two cultural and intellectual atmospheres. It may only reflect the possibility that the enduring problems of mankind are contemplated by different generations with similar hopes and apprehensions.

In addition to similarity of thought, proof should be provided that the later writer was in fact exposed to the ideas of the earlier one. Acknowledgment in the form of quotation and citation from or reference to the earlier work is therefore desirable. Absence of acknowledgment would not prove absence of influence, however; nor would acknowledgment prove its presence, for citation or reference to world figures like Confucius or Virgil, may be only for rhetorical effect — only to dress up an idea otherwise derived. To prove a veritable influence, it is necessary to show that the similar ideas thus dressed up would not have been born in the mind of the later thinker or would have had a different form or emphasis if they had not been generated or modified directly or indirectly by the supposed source.[30] And such a demonstration involves speculation upon how things might have happened if they had not in fact happened as they seem to have.

"Metahistorical" Speculation

The historian cannot evade such speculations by pretending that all he is interested in is what in fact happened, that an influence is established for him because he has documentary proof of it. Influences can rarely be established by documentary proof. No one can be a witness of *how* an influence has its effect; the witness can only record his opinion or judgment on that process. The trained historian ought not to judge *how* an influence was exerted, regardless of the quantity of evidence he may have on *what* happened, until he has satisfied himself by a process of elimination that the supposed influence did not come in some other way.

This kind of speculation involves what are sometimes called the *"ifs" of history* and may be properly called *metahistory*. It depends on judgments that are not "historicable." *Metahistory* is nevertheless not a negligible part of historical thought. To judge the significance, greatness, or influence of a person, thing, or event, one must ask what would have happened if he, she, or it had not been. That is as near as the historian can come to the process in the natural sciences whereby the investigator removes a factor in order to determine its function in an experiment.

---

[30] Cf. W. T. Jones, "The Term 'Influence' in Historical Studies," *Ethics*, LIII (1943), 192–201; also pp. 238–9 above.

Unfortunately, in our present state of knowledge it is probably impossible to establish objective criteria for such speculation in history. The historian can verify only happenings that have been recorded somehow. About others he can make only more or less debatable guesses. For that reason it is not his province to determine how much truth there might be in a generalization of which there are no recorded instances. E.g., "Ideas cannot be suppressed by force." If an idea has ever been thoroughly suppressed, the records of it must also have disappeared and hence the historian can know very little about it. The best he can do in testing such a generalization is only to examine the extent to which ideas that have been only partly suppressed by force — as, for example, those of the Carthaginians or the Waldenses — have nevertheless survived. That, of course, is not the same problem, though it is a very difficult one in itself. In other words, to be even "metahistorical," a problem has to have some kind of evidence or some kind of human experience associated with it. Totally vanished ideas, influences, and careers, are not in either category. They are in the realm of imaginative speculation or of wishful thinking, except that we may have some experience of how they may have vanished and how they may reappear.

Absolute Values vs. "Objective Relativism"

Recently an insistent clamor has arisen in certain quarters for fixed criteria in the evaluation of historical experience. It has occasionally taken the form of a demand for ethical values and absolutes. Obviously, if the historian were to know the *ought's* and *must-be's* of history, he could better judge the relative influence of individuals and the relative importance of particular ideas and events. Perhaps these historical absolutes are to be found in "the teachings of the Bible," "the hundred best books," "historical individuality," "the enduring charters of liberty," "the wisdom of the ages" — in other words, in the history of human aspirations expressed through religion, poetry, philosophy, art, and the great political manifestoes. Or, perhaps they are to be sought in the slow, painstaking, and apparently endless elaboration by social scientists of a social hygiene (which may well prove to be not far different from "the wisdom of the ages"). While that elaboration seems far off now, it is not without significance that Troeltsch, Meinecke, and Mannheim, leading students of changing ideas though they are, believe that absolute values may ultimately be attained.[31] And Beard has pointed out that the idea of historical relativity, if the relativists are right, must itself be relative, and therefore perhaps doomed to pass eventually.[32]

In the meantime, historians will have to write with such standards of value as they may have. It may be conceivable that some historians can discuss certain

---

[31] See above, pp. 111–12, n. 16. Cf. A. C. Benjamin, "The Scientific Status of Value Judgments," *Ethics*, LIII (1943), 212–18; E. S. Brightman *et al.*, "The Problem of an Objective Basis for Value Judgments," in *Science Philosophy and Religion: Third Symposium* (New York, 1943), pp. 1–11; and Philipp Frank *et al.*, "The Relativity of Truth and the Objectivity of Values," ibid., pp. 12–32.

[32] "Written History as an Act of Faith," p. 225.

subjects without betraying whether they consider them good or bad, beautiful or ugly. It is not conceivable that a serious historian will discuss anything without betraying whether he considers it true or untrue; and, as already indicated, he will not be able to select, arrange, or give proper emphasis to his exposition unless he has made some decision as to what is important and unimportant. It is, of course, possible that no necessary relationship connects the true with the good and the beautiful, and it unfortunately seems quite clear that the bad and the ugly may be important. Hence it appears theoretically possible for the historian to distinguish between the true and the untrue, the important and unimportant, by criteria independent of ethical and aesthetic values. Perhaps no historians have actually succeeded in doing so, however. If their values have not entered explicitly into their judgments, they have been implicit or unconscious. The question arises, therefore (and will soon be discussed) whether it is better to have a conscious set of values or to disclose them unconsciously.

Quantitative Measurements vs. Qualitative Guesses

Frustrated in the quest for objective criteria of value and influence, certain historians have attempted to apply quantitative measurements to such queries as whether the "great" books have been the influential ones. Faced, for example, with the controversies regarding the extent to which the American Revolution and the French Revolution were the result of French intellectual predominance, they have refused to rest content merely with the similarities in the later developments to the more significant among the earlier ideas. Hence they have tried to find numerical evidence of the spread of the writings of Montesquieu, Voltaire, Rousseau, and other *philosophes*. They have counted the editions of the *philosophes'* works, the number of times their separate writings are to be found in contemporary libraries, the frequency with which their books are quoted or cited by subsequent writers, and similar data.[33] This method provides a healthful corrective of the gratuitous assumption that books (which in this regard are not necessarily the same as the ideas they contain) have an influence proportionate to their merit. Nevertheless, it leaves much to be desired. To begin with, the presence of a book in a library does not indicate, on the one hand, that anyone read it or, on the other, that it was read by only one. Thus a book that appears once in library catalogues may have had a dozen readers while a book that appeared in a dozen libraries may have been read by no one. Furthermore, not everyone who reads a book is "influenced" by it; it may leave him totally unaffected, or it may provoke in him an unfavorable reaction.

In general, the unsuspecting must be warned, the influence of written works (perhaps not, however, including scientific reports) is easily overestimated. Influence, as has earlier been pointed out, is not neces-

---

[33] E.g., Daniel Mornet, *Les Origines Intellectuelles de la Révolution française* (1715–1787) (Paris, 1933); P. M. Spurlin, *Montesquieu in America*, 1760–1801 (University, La.; 1940). Cf. Louis Gottschalk "Philippe Sagnac and the Causes of the French Revolution," *Journal of Modern History*, XX (1948), 137–48.

sarily commensurate with popularity. Often the popular book only reflects rather than affects a prevalent contemporary attitude. This consideration, of course, makes those books which have truly influenced opinion the more significant to the historian of thought. All too often, however, neither influence nor popularity is a measure of aesthetic or ethical value, as an examination of almost any best seller list would tend to indicate.

The Problem of Unfavorable Reaction

An intriguing aspect of the problem of historical influence is that of *reaction against* an antecedent or contemporary person or event. Reactions to revolutionary movements, for example, have become so thoroughly conceptualized that it was possible for Trotsky to entitle a whole chapter [34] of his attack upon Stalin "The Soviet Thermidor," in the expectation that the reader would recognize the analogy to the Thermidorean Reaction following the Terror of the French Revolution. Similarly the rise and fall of a dictator followed by a restoration of the old authorities — as happened with Cromwell and Napoleon — has become a familiar pattern which helps to mold the expectations of students of revolutions. Such changes may be depicted on a graph of revolutionary developments as valleys of reaction following peaks of revolution. The political history of France from 1789 to our own day can easily be portrayed as a succession of such peaks and valleys. Some historians

[34] *The Revolution Betrayed* (Garden City, N.Y., 1937), Ch. V, pp. 86–114.

think also of the American Constitutional Convention of 1787 as a valley of reaction following an earlier revolutionary peak.

Reaction — that is, a tendency in the direction opposite to the applied pressure — is a personal as well as a social phenomenon. Only rarely does it happen that a leading personality, a great book, an original idea, a significant episode, or any other extraordinary human product creates among contemporaries only a favorable reaction, and when it does, one is usually safe in attributing the favor to the high degree of conformity of that product to the accepted cultural pattern. That is why a genuinely original achievement may be contemporaneously neglected or howled down and why it is sometimes said of a truly creative person that he "lived before his time." When ideas or persons seem far ahead of their day, they may have little or no effect either by direct influence or by reaction; they may be merely overlooked, perhaps to be better appreciated by subsequent generations.

But sometimes they have contemporary significance, both because a few welcome them and because others rise against them. The Waldenses, the Hussites, the Anabaptists, the English Chartists, the French Saint Simonians, the American Abolitionists and Prohibitionists, and the Russian Anarchists furnish excellent examples of movements that encountered such a dual reaction. It would be difficult to say whether the importance of such movements is greater as sources of favorable influence than as sources of irritation. Some might be one at one time and the other at another, and others might be both at the same time. At all events, *reaction against* antecedent and concurrent developments is a frequent and striking component of historical change. One is almost tempted to contend that in human affairs, as in physics, every action may be expected to have its reaction.

How to Prove an Influence

A recapitulation now seems in order of the considerations that may convincingly establish that one historical person, thing, or event (or groups thereof) had an influence upon another. (1) If A had an influence upon B, A must have been antecedent to or concurrent with B. For example, since it can be shown that the Prussian general Scharnhorst proposed revision of Prussia's military system before 1808, when a treaty with France limited the size of the Prussian army, it is obviously incorrect to attribute the origin of Scharnhorst's military reforms to that limitation; but it might be correct, if other evidence warrants, to attribute subsequent modifications of Scharnhorst's ideas to that limitation. (2) Similarity to A in thought or behavior on the part of B may also indicate influence, but is not sufficient in itself to do so. Nor does dissimilarity disprove influence, since the influence might have been a marked irritation or reaction resulting in a set of ideas or behavior not otherwise explicable. (3) Acknowledgment by B of A's influence may also be helpful in establishing it, but influences may operate effectively though unsuspected and therefore unacknowledged. If that were not true, much of the insidiousness of advertising and propaganda would be eliminated, and also the problem of historical relativism would be greatly simplified. On the other hand, an influence may be sincerely acknowledged and yet be more imagined than real, as is sometimes the case when persons display literary or artistic preferences and loyalties, or when writers use quotations for rhetorical effect. (4) Since all of these tests except that of time are inconclusive and time is conclusive only where an anachronism in the cause-and-effect sequence can be established, the best proof that B was influenced by A, where any evidence to that effect raises the probability, is to try to eliminate the other apparent causes of B's thought or action. Usually it will be found that other factors cannot be eliminated entirely. Hence, influence with rare exceptions is best conceived of as part of a complicated and not easily separable puzzle. Here again awareness of the intricacies at least makes the puzzle intelligible and may provide a good start toward a solution.

CHAPTER XI

THE HISTORIAN AND THE PROBLEMS OF THE PRESENT

It has been remarked that "a *Gesetzwissenschaft* employs a single case merely in order to help it to understand a general principle, whereas a *Geschichtswissenschaft* employs a general principle merely in order to help it understand a single case." [1] The importance of understanding general principles, of knowing whether the single cases with which they deal, fit into any generalization or typification, has often escaped the historian. That is why history is sometimes little more than mere antiquarianism, an effort to tell as complete a story as possible about something in the past that may have obvious interest to the historian though he is unable or does not feel called upon to explain why it should be of interest to anyone else. Fuller exploitation by historians of the social sciences in an effort to illustrate or test and to adapt or adopt the generalizations and classifications of sociologists, economists, and anthropologists has nevertheless been urged of late by some historians, notably among those of the United States. [2]

---

[1] Allport, p. 150.

[2] See, e.g., Roy F. Nichols, "Confusion in Historical Thinking," *Journal of Social Philosophy and Jurisprudence*, VII (1942), 334–43; Gottschalk, "Leon Trotsky and the Natural History of Revolutions," *loc. cit.*; *id.*, "Revolutionary Traditions and Analogies," *University [of Kansas City] Review*, VI (1939), 19–25; *id.*, "Causes

History and Social-Science Concepts

Despite persistent and widespread apprehensions, the use of social-science generalizations by the historian is increasing. It is not by accident, for instance, that there has recently been so much attention to urban, railroad, and business history, to the history of prices and of social thought, to the social and economic costs of war, and to the development of international institutions. The sphere of the historian's attention tends to be ruled by the law of supply and demand, and a demand by other disciplines for certain kinds of data encourages the historian to try to satisfy that demand. In so doing, he endeavors (1) to discover single cases that will illustrate a social-science generalization, (2) to discover single cases that will contradict a social-science generalization, and (3) to apply a social-science generalization to a historical trend or a series of similar events. In all three endeavors the historian, cooperating with the pertinent *Gesetzwissenschaften*, tries to modify, confirm, or take exception to a general idea borrowed from other social disciplines — usually with the hope that the sociological law will shed some light on the causal relationship among historical phenomena.

---

of Revolution," *American Journal of Sociology*, L (1944), 1–8; Ware, *Cultural Approach to History*, pp. 3–6; Crane Brinton, *Anatomy of Revolution*, pp. 11–37; Curti *et al*, pp. 138–40 (Propositions XV–XXI).

History as a Check on Sociological Generalizations

Finding contradictions in and exceptions to social-science generalizations is one of the ways the historian can best contribute to an understanding of society. It is easy for the generalizer to claim that the exceptions may only prove the rule. Occasionally, however, the exception may be the only way out of a logical rut. For some social-science concepts are based upon historical examples that the historian (or the social scientist as historian) has selected only because he was interested in or under the influence of that very concept. Marx, for example, with the French Revolution, the most influential of the revolutions before his day, foremost (though certainly not isolated) in his consciousness, came to the conclusion that class struggle was the essence of revolution. Under Marx's influence many subsequent historians have applied the concept of class struggle to other revolutions before and after, and have found that it fits. To that school of historians, class struggle has now become a part of revolution by definition: in so far as a movement departs from the preconceived pattern of a class struggle, it has been "betrayed" and is not a genuine revolution.[3] Thus a hermetical logical circle has been drawn.

Such an argument proceeds from premise to example and back to premise again. A single acceptable instance reinforces a concept; the concept leads to

---

[3] Cf. Daniel Guérin, *La Lutte de classes sous la Première République: bourgeois et "bras nus"* (1793–1797) (Paris, 1946) and Leon Trotsky, *The Revolution Betrayed* (New York, 1937).

the selection and interpretation of other examples; the accumulation of corroborating examples makes of the concept an intellectual convention. Allport's story will be recalled (see above p. 153) of the investigator who started from the hypothesis that radicalism-conservatism constitutes a first-order variable of personality and then had fifty students write autobiographies on that theme, and thus came within an ace of committing a similar logical fallacy. To be fully tested, a concept like that of revolution-as-class-struggle must be deliberately studied with a view to seeing whether valid contradictions and exceptions can be found in the past by historians. The risk is too great that it will not be adequately tested by revolutions in the future, because the convention will have become so generally accepted as to influence the pattern of future revolutions or, at any rate, the designation of future developments as revolutions. And besides the social scientist cannot afford to wait if there is a nearer road to a needed correction.

Much the same sort of process has been followed in the current concept of dictatorship. Edmund Burke, chiefly, it would appear, from the single example of Cromwell and from his own fearful logic, decided that military dictatorship must follow the upheaval of revolution. Now we look for — and, by the very expectation in the search, help to create social situations wherein we succeed in finding — dictators in the wake of revolutions. But if the generalization is wrong, we shall be able to discover its error only by seeking contradictions and exceptions, and to correct them only by modifications that make the

proper allowance for such contradictions and exceptions.

The historian thus becomes doubly useful to the
disciplines engaged in the effort to understand society.
He is not merely a purveyor of data to the social scientist; he also provides a check upon the validity of
social-science concepts for the past. Social scientists,
impatient with the historian who rejects their most
favored concepts because he knows exceptions, would
do well to remember that the health of a science depends upon its ability to withstand challenge to its
laws and to reject or revise those successfully challenged. And, on the other hand, historians should
bear in mind that one cannot even issue a proper
challenge if one does not appreciate the concept that
is under examination. It is taken for granted that a
historian ought not to write about the history, for
example, of theology or of physics without knowing
theology or physics. Too often, however, historians
have written about markets, business, and prices or
about personality and social behavior or about racial
and cultural attributes either without knowing the
findings of the relevant social scientists in those areas
of study or without making a choice among the frequently baffling conflicts of thought among them.

History and Psychology

An example may be ventured of an area of the
social sciences where progress may well be made easier
by deliberate and close coöperation with the historians. That is the field of *verstehende Psychologie* — the
psychological school of ideal types. Psychologists ac-

quainted with historical method and historians familiar with psychology techniques and principles
could, by the study of personality as illustrated by historical personages, make such a typology more authentic, more precise, and varied. As has been previously remarked (pp. 167–8) psychologist-historians
like these would have a distinct advantage over prac-
ticing psychologists in that their subjects, being dead,
could not act contrary to prediction, thus necessitat-
ing reclassification. Beginnings in the direction of
this kind of historical-psychological coöperation have
already been made.[4]

Historical Generalizations

Moreover, the historian should not (and, for all his
disclaimers, seldom does) hesitate to make his own
generalizations. If, examining writers A, B, C, and so
on, he finds that they have tended to be under the
influence of the climate of opinion prevailing in their
respective generations, he would be extraordinarily ob-
tuse or unduly wedded to his particulars if he failed
to conclude that writers in general tend to be influenced by the intellectual atmosphere of their day. If
he were to notice that argument after argument
against American slavery was humanitarian rather
than economic in nature, he would be falling short
of his scholarly duty not to conclude that the objection to slavery in America was humanitarian as well
as economic; and if his investigations were to continue into other kinds of slavery and reveal the same

---

[4] Kimball Young, *Personality and Problems of Adjustment* (New
York, 1940), pp. 320 and 323.

prevalence of humanitarian objections, he would be obliged as a historian to widen his generalization.

Some historians feel that their colleagues exceed their authority as historians when they draw generalizations of universal validity. Cautious historians would look askance at a bolder one who might state, for instance, that a number of past examples justifies the conclusion that wars *are more likely to occur* between neatly balanced alliances than between the weak and the strong. Such a conclusion would be universal, applicable to the future as well as the past; and his fellow-historians might feel that the member of the guild who had risked it was therefore going too far beyond the legitimate realm of history. Yet the same historians would not equally disapprove if their bolder colleague were to make some sort of generalization about the balance of power in the past. They would even be likely to approve if the institution or process involved in the generalization — unlike the recurrent problem of balance of power — were definitely past once and for all. The historian is in fact expected by other historians to make generalizations about the adequacy of ancient Roman political institutions, the economic character of feudalism, the limitations on royal authority in pre-Revolutionary France, the nature of nineteenth-century nationalism, or other persons, things, ideas, or events that are quite dead. If the boldly generalizing historian were to risk the concept that wars *have occurred in the past* more often between neatly balanced alliances than between the weak and the strong, the only quarrel of other historians would then be with his statistics.

Historical Types and Samples

Historians also commonly speak of *historical types and categories*, composites of traits belonging altogether perhaps to no one member of the group involved and yet considered characteristic of the group as a whole — such as "the Greek oracles," "the Roman patrician," "the Russian peasant," "the enlightened despot," "the Jacobin," "the American pioneer," etc. One of the things Lord Acton found so admirable in George Eliot's novels was her knack of "exposing scientifically and indifferently the soul of a Vestal, a Crusader, an Anabaptist, an Inquisitor, a Dervish, a Nihilist, or a Cavalier without attraction, preference or caricature." [5] It is her ability to portray historical types, not to create fictitious characters, that Acton here so enthusiastically appreciates. The historian, whenever he can, would prefer, however, to find a concrete *representative example* — a genuine historical figure who was more or less an average sample of his group. Nevertheless, it is chance rather than choice that determines the survival of historical records, and their chance nature seldom permits finding a good *representative example* and, still less, good "random sampling." As greater quantities of historical materials are now being more systematically preserved, it may become advisable in the future to use some sampling techniques in history. Today, however, the historian is more likely to employ the *example par excellence* — some individual who is so outstanding among his group that his atypical character provides an optimum

[5] Jan. 21, 1881, *Letters to Mary Gladstone*, p. 159.

or maximum for the estimation of the attitudes and behavior of the rest of his group. For example: "If Lafayette allowed his intendant to squeeze the peasants on his estates, less paternalistic landlords must have permitted their intendants to be even more demanding"; or: "Even Franklin D. Roosevelt before he died began to doubt the willingness of the Russians to keep their promises, and so it is not surprising that some of his subordinates were skeptical." *Historical types, representative examples, examples par excellence* are generalizations — in some instances, even generalizations from a single instance — but they are not frowned upon by historians so long as they are carefully documented and drawn from the past. It would thus appear that, in many instances, the acceptable historical generalization differs from the social-science concept only in tense.

The Utility of Historical Generalizations

Proposition XVI of the Committee on Historiography of the Social Science Research Council is to the effect that "historians may formulate generalizations of limited validity which are useful in the interpretation of the past until their modification is called for by new evidence." [6] The Committee cites as a hypothetical example of such a generalization "that the wasteful methods of early American farmers were due to a poor agricultural tradition rather than to their geographical or social environment." [7] It is not without importance that if this generalization is in fact

---

[6] Curti *et al.*, p. 138.
[7] Ibid., p. 140 n.

valid it provides to some degree at least an exception to another generalization — that of the "Turner thesis of United States history" to the effect that American culture was largely the product of influences encountered upon the successive frontiers. Thus, if true, it illustrates how continued historical investigation may be useful as a check upon earlier generalizations.

We shall return to this subject later (pp. 265–71). For the present it suffices to point out that no matter how hesitant the historian may be to extract rules for the prediction and control of the future, he is ready to make generalizations about the past. A few generalizations of that kind have been quite useful to the social scientist. Turner's frontier thesis, the work of Pirenne and Below on medieval urbanization, Bury's study of the idea of progress, Mahan's theory of the influence of sea power, the hypotheses on religious change of Renan and Troeltsch, the theories of Sombart, Weber, and Tawney on the origin of capitalism, and Toynbee's concept of the role of *challenge and response* in the creation of cultures are among them. In fact, it is sometimes hard to tell whether historians of ideas and institutions are historians rather than sociologists, particularly if they compare the ideas and institutions of several cultures; and probably it does not matter, if their work is well done.

The Value of Historical Method for the Social Scientist

The historian also makes a large number of generalizations of a methodological nature that students of society disregard to their disadvantage. Even

Thomas and Znaniecki used autobiographies and letters to newspapers without scrupulous inquiry into their authenticity or credibility; lesser social scientists sin more conspicuously in this regard. Social scientists more frequently than historians are guilty of the "misleading" questionnaire. They often tend also, still more than historians, to defer to government documents uncritically and to accept official histories without suspicion. Furthermore, they sometimes use secondary historical writings without careful analysis of their merits and sources of information or due consideration of conflicting schools of thought. For instance, a study of the natural history of revolution based exclusively on the liberal historians may well be criticized as one-sided. In fact, it has been remarked — perhaps not altogether justly — that whereas a historian seldom accepts a secondary account except as a starting point for a better one, a social scientist might accept it uncritically as a source of data. No one can reasonably expect a social scientist to derive his particulars from an analysis of the primary and original sources, but perhaps he ought to learn to be more critical of the "standard" secondary works of history.

The social scientist sometimes disregards historical information entirely. One occasionally has the feeling that he deals with familiar material in a complicated fashion — spending thousands of dollars to learn the location of houses of prostitution, as one cynic has put it — when earlier survivals or testimony might have revealed the desired information more simply. If the historians often betray a particularist passion for dryasdust antiquarianism, the sociologists are not altogether innocent of a preference for statistics, quanta, and measurements whose application seems to be fairly remote from both social utility and historical meaningfulness. Moreover, the historian sometimes has an uneasy feeling that some sociological generalization involving types or cycles are at best "hunches" or figures of speech rather than working hypotheses.[8]

Occasionally, too, the social scientist makes less allowance for the egocentrism of compilers of quantitative than for those of qualitative data. The use of compilations like the *Encyclopædia Britannica*, for example, to measure scientific achievement (by the number of lines assigned to each subject) is perhaps forgivable in view of the relative lack of other norms;[9] but such apparently quantitative measurements are in fact largely qualitative. The same holds true also of units of war, revolution, etc., when definitions of both the units of measurements and the things measured are debatable and variable. It is no extenuation for the sociologist, lamentable though it is, that the historian,

---

[8] Cf. Louis Gottschalk, "Potentialities of Comparative History," *Bulletin of the Society for Social Research*, XV (1936) and "A Critique of Sorokin's *Social and Cultural Dynamics*," ibid., XVII (1939); also Edward Shils, *The Present State of American Sociology* (Glencoe, Ill., 1945), p. 62.

[9] Sorokin (II, 143 and 152) goes to great pains to point out that the *Encyclopædia Britannica* gives disproportionate space to English and to recent scientists, and that space-measurements derived from it must therefore have a large qualitative content. See also his strictures on the use of quantitative measurements in his review of Quincy Wright, *A Study of War* (2 vols.; *Chicago*, 1942) in *Ethics*, LIII (1943), 204. Nevertheless Sorokin uses such data frequently.

in his turn, frequently uses quantitative language (e.g., words like *often, great, very, significant*) without realizing that he is doing so.

Precaution Regarding Historical Generalizations

A historical generalization cannot be tested, as can a generalization in the physical sciences or even, on occasion, in the social sciences, by controlled experimentation. As has already been said, the historian knows no process quite like that of the laboratory by which one can remove from or add to an experiment one or more ingredients or factors to determine their effect. Therefore he cannot apply practical tests to his generalizations. So far as this can be done at all in history, it has to be done either by applying the imagination to the "ifs" and the "might-have-beens" of history (as explained above in connection with "meta-history") or by comparing and contrasting similar categories of historical developments (such as wars, dictatorships, urban growth, and frontier settlements) in an effort to discover and account for similarities and dissimilarities. Such parallels, however, no matter how skillfully applied, fall far short of actual observation. To this shortcoming must be added the complexities of human affairs — e.g., the unsolved problem of determinism and free-will, the misunderstood and perhaps not understandable role of accident in history,[10] the highly debatable place to be assigned to personality and leadership, the changing social atmosphere from place to place and from generation to

---

[10] Cf. Sidney Hook, "Chance, Accident and Contingency," in Curti *et al.*, pp. 115–16; and above, pp. 210–11.

generation. Furthermore, the historian can never be sure he knows all the facts pertinent to any set of historical phenomena with which he is concerned, since many of them, it may be assumed, are irrevocably lost. Hence, whatever generalization a historian may make must be based upon experimentally inadequate, numerically incomplete, and largely non-objective data. Such generalizations must be regarded as having only limited validity and being subject to rapid correction as more data or more valid points of view dictate correction.

The Problem of Prediction

Moreover, a phenomenon that applies uniquely to human beings makes it preferable for the historian to limit his generalizations to past events and institutions: the very fact that a generalization regarding the past behavior of human beings is considered correct may in and of itself lead to a new pattern of behavior calculated to avoid the bad or increase the good implicit in the generalization. The careful historian ought to limit himself merely to stressing one among several possible outcomes when a current situation appears analogous to a past one. Too many unknowns should cause him to be cautious about prognosticating more emphatically. Even technological experts, where the human mind is one of the factors to be considered, have to proceed cautiously, as the atomic scientists have recently discovered, in their prognostications. Yet the historian engages in two kinds of operations — already broached (pp. 256–7 and 260) — that may aid others to make predictions and have emboldened less cautious historians sometimes themselves to venture predictions. Those two operations are the drawing of *historical analogies* and the tracing of *historical trends*. They correspond roughly to history as statics (comparatively considered) and history as dynamics, or, to use an older terminology, comparisons of "cross-sections of history" and "longitudinal sections of history."

Anticipation on the Basis of Precedent

By placing similar cross-sections of history side by side, the historian can find contrasts and comparisons among them. Isolating the comparables, he can endeavor to determine what makes them comparable. On the major premise that like consequences are derived from like antecedents, he may deduce that comparable circumstances in the future may be followed by comparable consequences. In less academic circles, such deductions would be called "the lessons of history." Thucydides, we have seen, wrote his history to teach such lessons; and Thomas Jefferson considered this didactic potential of history the core of the education of citizens: "History by apprizing them of the past, will enable them to judge the future; it will avail them of the experience of other times and other nations; it will qualify them as judges of the actions and designs of men." [11]

Jefferson was perhaps too optimistic. A patent weakness in this process of reasoning lies in the variability

---

[11] See above, p. 213; *Notes on Virginia* in A. A. Lipscomb and A. E. Bergh, *The Writings of Thomas Jefferson* (Washington, 1905), I, 207.

of ideas of historical causation discussed above (pp. 212–22). That weakness is somewhat compensated for when one deals with a set of analogous examples all in the past, since the consequences are known and the antecedents may be inferred from the consequences. For the historian is in a position where he can recognize a consequence best by reasoning backward from consequent to antecedent. As soon as today becomes yesterday and tomorrow today, he feels competent to explain why whatever happened yesterday or today must inevitably have happened, but he does not consider it his business to attempt to guess what the inevitable will be tomorrow. It may be, as the White Queen said to Alice, that "it's a poor sort of memory that only works backwards," but it's the kind historians cultivate. When the consequents are not yet clearly ascertainable, the antecedents can be only dimly seen and none but a bold historian would dare to make a prediction.

And yet it would seem that if a generalization is true for the past, it ought to be true *within limits* for the future. For instance, the striking parallel of the French Revolution with the English Revolution a century earlier did not escape contemporaries like Benjamin Constant and Armand Carrel, and they were able to make shrewd guesses as to what might happen to Napoleon and to the restored Bourbons. It was possible during the Second World War for the Army Air Force Committee of Historians to predict that since, in 1806 and 1918, Prussia had collapsed rapidly after but not before military defeat, *one of the possibilities* to anticipate after another military defeat, but not earlier, was the rapid collapse of Germany. It should be stressed that this was no further in the realm of prediction than *anticipation* of one of several possible outcomes. Regardless of historical precedent, the rapid collapse of Prussia would have been *one of the future possibilities* in any event. But *historical analogy* gave the anticipation a greater degree of persuasiveness than it might otherwise have had. On the other hand, if it had been predicted that, merely because there were historical precedents to that effect, Germany *must* collapse rapidly upon military defeat, the prediction might have appeared too bold and might not have carried conviction. It would too patently have overlooked other factors that ought to have entered into the calculation. Those factors included not only the differences in the scenes, circumstances, and personalities, but also — and more importantly — the fact that the Nazis too, by the same process of historical analogy, had learned the lesson of 1918 and could have been counted upon to take precautions to circumvent collapse upon military defeat. As a matter of fact, the Nazis did just that and succeeded in postponing collapse until their military defeat had become total.[12]

The Nazis' use of "anticipation from historical precedent" in this instance might serve as a practical example of its effectiveness for control, if not for pre-

[12] The student might find it a useful exercise in "historical anticipation" to compare the earlier version of this paragraph with the present one. See Louis Gottschalk *et al.*, *The Use of Personal Documents in History, Anthropology and Sociology* ("Social Science Research Council Bulletin #53") (New York, 1945), p. 70 and n. 8.

diction. Another example of the practical use of historical analogy is furnished by Napoleon Bonaparte. He is said to have consistently included among his preparations for a campaign a careful study of the history of the most recent campaigns in the same theatre of war.[13] But if he had been content to do only that, he could readily have been outwitted by any general who acted contrary to recognized military precedents; and the general who knew least about the precedents would logically have proved to be his ablest opponent. Yet that he could win battles by doing what the successful generals before him had done on the same fields and by avoiding the errors of the unsuccessful ones was at least one of the possibilities that could be *anticipated*. On similar suppositions war colleges study the history of past wars.

"I know of no way of judging the future but by the past," Patrick Henry is reported as having said in a speech to the Virginia Convention in 1775. That was a fitting remark by one who is supposed to have thought that George III might profit by the examples of Brutus and Caesar, Cromwell and Charles I. Yet, despite all his knowledge of Caesar and Charles, Henry would have been unable to tell whether George III would or would not profit by their examples. For that he needed skills other than those of the historian. History alone was not enough for prediction; but it was helpful. George III might have profited by example! And so might Napoleon have profited by the

---

[13] Spencer Wilkinson, *The Rise of General Bonaparte* (Oxford, 1930), p. 149.

example of the Russian invasion of Charles XII of Sweden, and Hitler by the example of Napoleon.

The trouble with historical parallels as a means of prognostication is that, while it is fairly clear that human beings *can* learn from history, they can be *counted upon neither to do so nor not to do so.* If they should learn, the chances of their doing the same thing over if it is desirable, or avoiding doing it if it is undesirable, are good. But since they cannot be counted upon, historical analogies present us most often with clues to *possible* rather than *probable* behavior, with the ability only to *anticipate* rather than to *predict,* to *take precautions* rather than to *control.* Proposition XVIII of the Committee on Historiography of the Social Science Research Council underlines this point:

Many large questions of public interest cannot be answered conclusively out of historical knowledge, and historians true to the scientific spirit will avoid encouraging the pretentions that they can be so answered. In certain and limited cases, however, by the use of historical knowledge and analogies, the historian may, in respect of given situations, indicate various contingencies, one or more of which may be anticipated with a high degree of probability.[14]

Extrapolation of Historical Trends

That there has been fairly continuous development (not necessarily improvement, however) in various activities of mankind seems an inescapable assumption. Despite possible gaps, a steady continuity can

---

[14] Curti *et al.,* p. 139.

be traced in the growth of capitalism, the development of a revolutionary tradition, the accumulation of ideas of war and peace, the rise and fall of monarchism, the rise and fall of prices, the spread of various business practices and social institutions, etc. If the course of such developments can be correctly described for the past, can it be safely extrapolated into the near future? The economists, largely on the basis of historical knowledge, have succeeded within limits with the extrapolation of the business cycle. Is there similarly a war cycle, a peace cycle, a revolutionary cycle? Sorokin and Quincy Wright have attempted to answer such questions. Neither may think of himself as merely a historian, but the historian dares not disregard the kind of question they raise. Can history shed light on problems like personality, social change, the sociology of knowledge, culture lag, ethical and aesthetic values?

The historian has often been content to leave such questions to the philosopher and the social scientists. When governments seek advice on social trends or on planning, they ask political scientists, sociologists, or economists to prepare reports, but they seldom ask historians. For historians on the whole prefer, and are more or less obliged by the demanding nature of their research, to do their work within limited chronological periods and restricted geographical areas beyond which they hate to trespass in order to trace long-term continua and trends or analogies. When a historian like Toynbee undertakes to arrange the history of several civilizations by hypotheses or categories of enduring problems rather than by periods and areas, the social scientists and philosophers are more ready to heed him than are his fellow historians.

When the historian shies away from such efforts out of fear that no one person can expertly master so large a field as the whole of man's past, his instinct is perhaps justified. But sometimes, as Dr. Arnold's comment quoted above [15] suggests, the historian is too often interested in things that are dead and no longer matter, whether remote or near in time, to the neglect of the enduring problems, achievements, and values of mankind. Antiquarianism and an interest in the past for the sake of the past are highly commendable no doubt, and society can be expected to support more than a few historians for archival, museum, and pedagogical purposes. But, no matter how regrettable it may seem, society is also bound to ask of the historian (especially if he is also a teacher in our schools and colleges) how he otherwise can socially justify his expenditure of time and money; and the answer ought to have some relation to the understanding of contemporary man and his problems. It would be unfortunate for historical scholarship if the teaching of the history of some significant periods in specified areas were abandoned, but cannot greater room be found than is at present available for significant problems, institutions, and developments that over long periods and in several places have engaged man's attention and may be expected to do so again?

---

[15] P. 203.

"Contemporaneity of Evidence"

We have already seen the importance to the historian of trying to understand persons and events in their own setting, their "contemporary past" (pp. 136–8). The historian also tries to reach understanding by examining his subject from the vantage point of his own present. This is a process similar to those which the psychologists call *insight* and *discerning.*[16] Having amassed as many pertinent details as he can about a past happening, the historian brings all his knowledge and personal experience to bear upon them in order to help him see the relationship among them. Thus he makes a *psychological analogy* (or contrast) between his own mental reactions to his own experience (including vicarious experience, i.e., reflection upon experience of others) and the mental reactions of past figures to the past experiences under study.[17] This totality of his own experience is his substitute for, or "empirical equivalent" of, the totality of the past that has perished. Only by such an analogy (or contrast) can he understand the setting of the testimony of his sources and the behavior to which it testifies. This can be carried to the point where the historical past can be incorporated into the living memory of the historian, becoming almost as real to him as his own past. That is what is meant in part by the "presentist" approach to history. Some philosophers and philosophically inclined historians

---

[16] Allport, pp. 152–3.

[17] Blumer (p. 74) maintains that Thomas and Znaniecki derived their primary theoretical schemes in a similar fashion.

contend that all living history is contemporaneous, that it is "contemporary thought about the past," or "the specious present," or "the re-enactment of past experience." [18]

Differing Approaches to History

To this kind of understanding of the past in terms of the present must also be added the contention of the same school of thought that present interests determine the historian's *choice of what is worth studying* in the past as well as the librarian's and archivist's *choice of what records are worth preserving* and the publisher's *choice of what is worth printing*. Because each nation understands the past in the light of its own experience and because each nation is interested in the origin and development of different things, we have varying national histories. Anyone who doubts that the same historical facts can be honestly (though not necessarily scientifically) interpreted in drastically different fashions by reputable scholars of different nationalities ought to compare, for example, Canadian and United States accounts of the War of 1812, or Mexican and United States accounts of the Vera Cruz episode of 1914. And successive generations for

---

[18] The three quoted phrases are respectively from Beard, *loc cit.*, p. 219; Becker, "Every Man His Own Historian," *loc. cit.*, pp. 226–7; and Collingwood, p. 282. Cf. Croce, *op. cit.*; R. V. Burks, "Benedetto Croce" in B. E. Schmitt (ed.), *Some Historians of Modern Europe, Essays in Historiography by Former Students of the Department of History at the University of Chicago* (Chicago, 1942), pp. 66–99; F. J. E. Woodbridge, *The Purpose of History* (New York, 1916); V. G. Simkhovitch, "Approaches to History," *Political Science Quarterly*, XLIV (1929), 484–5; Collingwood, pp. 205–315; Sidney Hook, "Understanding," in Curti *et al.*, p. 130.

similar reasons reinterpret the past and rewrite history. Even "Orphan Annie" learned that from her history teacher: "It's human nature to write what's popular in each generation, I guess." [19] This does not mean that the "facts" change; it does mean that what is considered worthy of selection and emphasis changes, and perhaps too, theories as to how they came about.

Sometimes it takes less than a generation for the dominant theme to change. A history of Europe since 1914 written before 1930 might very well have had as its central theme the struggle for collective security. By 1939 that central theme would have become clearly a pious hypothesis, permitting only a partial and one-sided presentation of the salient events of the intervening decade, which led away from collective security to the Second World War. In 1945 it was possible to hope that the striving for collective security might again stand forth as the central thread of European history since 1914.[20] A few years later one wondered whether the theme of *raison d'état* and power politics or the rise of atomic physics might not be more appropriate. Studies of recent history (except where they are only new printings of old books with supplementary chapters meant to bring them up to date) are more or less bound to center around the origins and background of the most striking and palpable developments of the day. A turn in events a decade or a century hence may make some unno-

[19] Harold Gray, strip of March 13, 1946, News Syndicate Company, Inc.
[20] Cf. Louis Gottschalk *et al.*, p. 68.

ticed and vaguely recorded facts of our time the very ones about which the historian of that day will be most inquisitive. What seems negligible in the "becoming" may look vital in the "become."

Analogies of the Past with the Present

The influence of the present upon the understanding of the past is, however, even more subtle than these obvious illustrations indicate. Contemporary events not only determine our guesses as to what trends form the central core of history; by the process that we have called the *historical analogy* they also affect our understanding of the past events of a similar nature. To a historian who has lived through historical crises, earlier crises take on added significance. For example, provided he does not push the analogy too far, his own experience with the inflation of the 1920's or of the 1940's should make the effects of inflation in eighteenth-century France and America easier for the historian to understand; Hitler's New Order should shed a revealing light on Napoleon's Continental System; Stalinism should help to make Caesarism and Bonapartism more intelligible; and *vice versa*. One who has experienced war, depression, and revolution may be better able to interpret war in the ancient Mediterranean world, may examine more comprehendingly the depressions in the Roman imperial period, may more fully understand revolutionary excess and counter-revolutionary intrigue in post-Renaissance times. This does not mean that past inflations, autarkies, wars, depressions, and revolutions are necessarily just like more recent ones. They may easily be unlike. It does mean that such concepts cannot be grasped by the historian except by reconstructive imagination. A past inflation or autarky or war can be meaningful to him only as it is like or unlike a concept of the same kind in his mind.

The Past in the Light of the Present

To recapitulate, there are at least three ways in which the present determines how the historian will interpret the past. The first of these is derived from the inescapable tendency to understand others' behavior, and hence others' testimony, in the light of one's own behavior patterns; this results in *psychological analogies* (or contrasts) between the historian's mental processes and those of the historical personalities whom he studies. The second is due to the fact that his own intellectual climate is a deciding factor in the historian's *choice* of subjects for investigation (not to mention the availability, selection, and arrangement of his data). The third comes from his exploitation of current events in lieu of a laboratory; from the episodes and developments of his own day he draws *historical analogies* to the episodes and developments of the past. Thus history becomes "the living past," the memory of living man, meaningful to him but having little objective reality except in so far as it is confirmable by a critical analysis of surviving testimony. "The events of history do not 'pass in review' before the historian. They have finished happening before he begins thinking about them. He has to re-create them inside his own mind, re-enacting for himself so much of the experience of the men who took part in them as he wishes to understand." [21]

In short, whether or not the past helps us to understand the present, the present inevitably colors our understanding of the past. So true is that — so nearly inescapable is the learning process by which we proceed from the known (our own experience) to an understanding of the unknown (the past) — that the historian must be constantly on guard against identifying movements and institutions of the past with contemporary ones, as did Taine in transferring his hatred of Communists and Communards to *philosophes* and Jacobins, and as frequently contemporary commentators do who too closely identify Stalin with Hitler and Napoleon.[22] Against such half-true transferences of identity the historian has only one defense. *Historical-mindedness* (see pp. 136–8), the studied effort to understand the past in its own setting, acts as a check upon both the *historical* and the *psychological analogy*.

The Scientific Spirit in History

Because generalizations regarding historical facts must be regarded as of limited validity, because any causal scheme applied to history is apt to have a large element of personal bias, and because the understanding of history has to be viewed as an effort of a mind conditioned by a present culture, it is sometimes contended that any interpretation of history is as good

---

[21] Collingwood, p. 97.

[22] Cf. Louis Gottschalk, "How Evaluate the Russian Revolution," *Common Cause*, III (1950), 434–9.

as any other and no criterion of historical validity is demonstrably superior to any other. Such a contention disregards several principles that the conscientious historian generally endeavors to practice.

In the first place, the scholarly historian feels under obligation to distinguish between problems that are "historicable" and those that are not. Certain questions, though they concern the past of mankind, cannot be answered by an analysis of historical survival and testimony. (1) Prominent among these are questions involving value judgments (already discussed on pp. 110 and 242–5). Whether policies, persons, institutions, or human achievements are good or bad, right or wrong, ugly or beautiful, great or petty is not a matter to which anyone can testify except as to his own and, to a limited extent, others' *opinions* regarding them. (2) In addition, an estimate of the *ifs* of history is, at best, a good guess and hardly verifiable by evidence. (3) Likewise, whether one's interpretation of cause, influence, and motivation is correct may be a matter of inner conviction rather than of logical inference from testimony and is therefore often (but not necessarily) highly debatable. The fact that the historian to be meaningful has to have standards of ethics and aesthetics and some kind of frame of reference does not mean that his standards and philosophies, even when they are explicit, can be acquired by a strict application of the historical method. In these areas the scientific spirit is demonstrated by a readiness to understand the limitations (and the potentialities) of the historical method in helping to make a choice and to recognize the margin that may remain for justifiable disagreement.

Likewise, where questions are "historicable," the historian respectful of the scientific spirit feels certain scholarly practices incumbent upon him. (1) He will feel under obligation to collect all the important relevant data he can find bearing upon his problem in the hope that a definite judgment may ultimately be justified. (2) As conscientiously as possible, he will try to give to each piece of testimony in his collected data its full and no more than its full weight. (3) He will also make a conscious effort to lean over backward against his own national, religious, racial, party, class, professional, or other biases. In this connection, Lord Acton's instruction to the contributors to the *Cambridge Modern History* remains a goal, no matter how unrealizable in practice: to write as if established "in Long. 30° W." [23] — that is, in the middle of the Atlantic Ocean in complete social isolation. (4) In cases where the testimony is unavailable or, if available, inadequate for a definite conclusion, he will be careful not to give definite answers but to suspend judgment. (5) Finally, he will studiously avoid gratuitous assumptions or inferences and will endeavor to present only such conclusions as logically proceed from the evidence that he has presented. [24]

Even the strictest application of these principles

---

[23] March 12, 1898, *Lectures on Modern History* (London, 1906), p. 318.

[24] Cf. Curti *et al.*, p. 134.

280 UNDERSTANDING HISTORY

and the strictest accountability to his scientific obligations will not eliminate the conditioned, subjective,
and "presentist" reactions of the historian but, no
matter how weak the flesh, they furnish standards for
testing his scientific spirit.

APPENDIX

RULES

For the Guidance of
Authors and Translators*

One item in the cost of book-manufacture that is often large
and avoidable is the expense of resetting because the manuscript from which the printer worked was incorrect or illegible. Time, trouble, and expense can be saved if authors
and translators take care to see that the manuscript sent to
the printer is letter-perfect — that names, dates, figures, and
other facts are correct, that the text is consistent in punctuation and style, that the phrasing is in its final form, just as
the writer wishes it. When alterations in proof are necessary,
their cost, which is greater than inexperienced writers usually
anticipate, can be reduced if, by counting letters and spaces,
the new material is made to fit as nearly as possible the space
of the material deleted.

Uniformity in usage is more important than adherence to
any given style. Spelling, punctuation, hyphenation, and
other such typographical details should be consistent throughout the manuscript, to avoid embarrassing and costly queries
from the printer's proof-room.

Copy (matter to be set by the compositor) should be typewritten on one side only of paper of about eight by eleven
inches, with a margin of at least an inch and a half at each
side. The text, *including footnotes and any special matter
intended to be set in smaller type*, should be double-spaced.
Avoid hyphenating words at the end of lines where easily
possible. Any necessary handwritten alterations should be in
ink and plainly legible. Pages should be numbered consecu-

---

* Prepared by Raymond A. Preston of Alfred A. Knopf, Inc.

tively throughout, not those of each chapter separately. Inserted pages should be numbered alphabetically: 11 A, 11 B, etc., and the words "Pages 11 A, 11 B, follow" inserted at the foot of the preceding page. Where pages are taken out, notice should be given on the preceding page; for example, on page 11 the words: "Page 20 follows."

Front matter, such as title page, dedication, table of contents, list of illustrations, etc., should accompany the manuscript.

Manuscript should never be rolled or folded.

Authors should keep a duplicate of the manuscript, for reference and to safeguard against loss, but the manuscript for the printer's use should, whenever possible, be the original ribbon copy, not a carbon or mimeographed copy.

SPELLING

For books to be published with American spelling the best authority is *Webster's New International Dictionary*, second edition (G. & C. Merriam Co., Springfield, Mass., publishers), of which *Webster's Collegiate Dictionary* is a useful abridgment. (Spell, however, *kidnapper, kidnapped, kidnapping, worshipper, worshipped, worshipping*, so, regardless of Webster.) For books with English spelling the best authority is *A New English Dictionary on Historical Principles*, edited by Sir James Murray, and generally referred to as the *Oxford Dictionary*; or its abridgment, *The Concise Oxford Dictionary of Current English*, adapted by H. W. and F. G. Fowler.

For proper names of persons and places, follow the *New International* so far as it contains them. *Webster's Biographical Dictionary* and *Webster's Geographical Dictionary* are useful and authoritative reference books.

The possessive case of proper names in the singular, whether ending in *s* or not, should be formed by adding *'s*: *Charles's, Dickens's.* (*Jesus'* and ancient classical and Biblical proper names in *s* are exceptions: e.g., *Venus', Moses', Pericles'.*)

A ligature is indicated in manuscript by a curved stroke

connecting the two letters of the dipthong: *formulǽ*, *for-mulæ*; *ŒEdipus*, *Œdipus*; *Cǽsar*, *Cæsar*.

PUNCTUATION

An excellent brief summary of the best contemporary practice in punctuation is contained in C. H. Ward's *What Is English?* (Scott, Foresman and Company, Chicago, publishers). On this and many other matters of concern to writers, among the innumerable reference works that might be cited, *A Dictionary of Modern English Usage*, by H. W. Fowler (see article "Stops" for punctuation) (Oxford University Press), and *Words into Type*, based on studies by Marjorie E. Skillin, Robert M. Gay, and others (New York: Appleton-Century-Crofts), are recommended.

A comma should be placed before the *and* when *and* is used between only the last two members of a series of three or more co-ordinate words or phrases: "the red, white, and blue."

Use no period after the contractions *Mme*, *Mlle*; but do not omit it after *M.*, *Mr.*, *Mrs.*, etc.

When an expression like "He said" or "She replied" is used to introduce a direct quotation, use a colon, not a comma, before the quoted matter.

Three points separated by en quadrats (. . .) mark an omission of words, from a conversation, or in editing or translating. (At the end of a declaratory sentence the period makes an additional, fourth, point.) Such points are also often used to indicate a suspension, pause, or sudden turn in the thought, for which a dash would be more suitable. This practice has been so overdone that caution should be exercised in using points of omission for this purpose.

Use double quotation marks ("quotes") for ordinary quoted matter, single "quotes" for a quotation within a quotation. Should there be a third quotation within the second, use double "quotes" again; and so on. Do not start with single "quotes." This applies to all direct discourse, whether spoken or thought. There is no sound reason for beginning direct discourse after "he thought," for instance, with single "quotes" when double "quotes" would follow "he said."

As for the order of punctuation marks when used in combination with "quotes," a period or a comma should always precede the closing quotation mark; a semicolon or a colon should always follow the closing quotation mark; an exclamation mark or a question mark should precede or follow the closing quotation mark according as the exclamation mark or question mark is or is not part of the quotation. Thus: "Did he say: 'I told you so'?" "He said: 'Didn't I tell you so?' "

After Roman numerals do not use a period, except at the end of a sentence. Thus, write: "Louis XVI was executed."

Hyphens. In no matter is English so unsettled as in the use of hyphens. *The Concise Oxford Dictionary*, Fowler's *Dictionary of Modern English Usage*, and *Webster's New International Dictionary* are good authorities. But whatever system is followed, it is generally helpful to connect by a hyphen a verbal noun (gerund) with a noun it modifies. The hyphen differentiates between a "waiting room" and a "waiting-room," between a "walking stick" and a "walking-stick."

Note that the use of the hyphen sometimes depends on the position of words in the structure of the sentence or on their meaning; thus, "a well-known man," but "a man well known." Usually when an adjective (or participle) and a noun are used in combination adjectivally, a hyphen should connect them: "a poverty-stricken man," "a twentieth-century book." Other such unit modifiers, as they are called, are generally recognized to require a hyphen for the sake of clearness. Adverbs in *-ly* should almost never be so connected: "A beautifully printed book."

Use a hyphen to distinguish between *re-create* and *recreate*, *re-creation* and *recreation*.

For syllabication, follow *Webster's New International Dictionary*, except that no division should be made between *q* and *u*. In dividing a word at the end of a line, hyphenate according to pronunciation, not according to derivation. Thus: *antith-esis*, not *anti-thesis*; *hypoth-esis*, not *hypo-thesis*; *knowl-edge*, not *know-ledge*; *philos-ophy*, not *philo-sophy*.

Dashes. The ordinary dash, an "em" dash, is used to indicate a break in a sentence, either within it or at the end. To denote this dash in a manuscript, it is generally sufficient to use two typewritten hyphens. An "en" dash, half as long as an "em" dash, and about twice as long as a hyphen, is used to join two numbers indicating the beginning and end of a series. For example, "the years 1830–40," "pages 247–60," should be marked as follows in a typewritten manuscript:

$$1830\frac{/}{in}\text{-}40 \quad \text{pages} \quad 247\frac{/}{in}\text{-}60$$

In such instances use the fewest figures that will suffice; for example, "1830–40," not "1830–1840"; but "11–19," "1911–12," and other figures between 11 and 19 inclusive.

Do not use a comma or a colon in combination with a dash.

NUMBERS

No rigid rule can be given for spelling out numbers or using figures. Much depends on context. In general it may be said that small and simple numbers and round numbers should be spelled out; dates are best expressed in figures. Where comparative numbers are given — as, for example, in stating a growth in population, the rise or fall in prices, or sports scores — and the reader is expected to do a simple mathematical problem in his head, figures are more helpful. Thus: "The population increased from 2,453 in 1900 to nearly 5,600 in 1910."

Use the forms "the nineties" (no apostrophe), "the 1890's."

No hyphen is needed in "nine tenths" — any more than in "nine cents."

In bibliographical work use roman capitals for volume numbers, lower-case roman for chapter numbers, and arabic figures for page numbers. Thus, "Volume II, Chapter ii, page 2," regardless of the usage of the work referred to.

ITALICS

Words and phrases in foreign languages should be italicized unless they are regarded as Anglicized. *Webster's New International Dictionary* is an excellent authority on this matter. In works that require many foreign words for which there are no English equivalents, it is better, however, to print single words in roman type, unless, perhaps, on their first appearance, and phrases in italic.

Care should be taken to insert correct accents in foreign words. German and Danish nouns italicized as foreign must have a capital initial. Do not supply English plurals for words italicized as foreign.

Names of ships should be italic.

Words used as words — for instance, "the word *man*" — should be in italic or else enclosed in quotation marks. Whichever practice is chosen, it should be followed throughout the book.

Italicize the names of books and periodicals. The article should be italicized if it is part of the title of a book, but not of a periodical: *The Tempest*, the *New York Times*. Use roman type and quotation marks for chapter titles referred to, subdivisions of works, titles of individual articles, essays, or poems that form part of a volume, and unpublished theses.

The abbreviations cf., e.g., etc., et seq., ib., ibid., i.e., loc. cit., q.v., s.v., viz., should ordinarily be printed in roman. *Ante, c. (circa), infra, passim, post,* and *supra* should be printed in italics.

ABBREVIATIONS

Except for the usual *M., Mr., Mrs.,* and *Dr.,* avoid abbreviations in literary texts. They may be more freely used in footnotes, but even there caution is necessary. Abbreviations for the titles of learned periodicals, for instance, at least the first time they are cited, are an annoyance to the lay reader unacquainted with them.

In bibliographical notes, *ibid., loc. cit.,* and *op. cit.* (not italicized) may be used to avoid repetition and save space, but care must be exercised to use them properly and to avoid ambiguity. *Ibid.* ("the same") refers to a single work cited in the preceding note or to a work referred to in the text with the corresponding footnote reference figure attached. If more than one work is referred to in the preceding note, the title should be repeated. *Loc. cit.* (for *loco citato,* "in the place cited") refers to a previously cited work by the same authors in a periodical or in a book by more than one author. *Op. cit.* (for *opere citato,* "in the work cited") refers to a volume by the same author previously cited.

Good academic usage now tries to avoid the sometimes confusing *op. cit.* and *loc. cit.* Citations after the first reference give the author's last name and a shortened title, with *ibid.* used to avoid repetition.

The abbreviations *a.m.* (*ante meridiem,* "before noon") and *p.m.* (*post meridiem,* "after noon") should be in lower-case roman type. B.C. ("before Christ") and A.D. (*anno Domini,* "in the year of our Lord") should be in small capitals, roman, the former following a date, the latter preceding a date. Thus, "432 B.C.," "A.D. 1564."

CAPITALIZATION

For the use of capitals *Webster's New International Dictionary* is a good authority. As in other matters, where authorities differ, uniform and consistent usage throughout a book is to be striven for, whatever authority is followed.

Capitalize government titles and titles of nobility when referring to specific individuals, as "The President was born in 1882"; but not when referring to an office or title in general: "The president of the United States has more power than the king of England."

Capitalize *East, West, North, South,* and the corresponding derivatives when they refer to political divisions, as *Western Australia, North Holland,* or to parts of the United States, as *Southern, Easterner,* the *Northwest,* and not merely to points of the compass, as in: "He went west," "western Europe." Capitalize *East, West,* when referring to the Orient, the Occident.

Do not capitalize *rue*, *boulevard*, *faubourg*, etc., when used with proper names: *rue Duphot*, *faubourg Saint-Germain*.

A, AN

Use *a* rather than *an* before words beginning with *h* in which the *h* is sounded, whether the first syllable is accented or not; for example, "a historical," "a heroic"; but "an hour."

FOOTNOTES

Footnotes, as well as the main text, should be double-spaced, to allow room for interlinear alterations if necessary. A footnote in manuscript may be inserted immediately after the line in which reference to it is made, with rules drawn across the page above and below to separate it from the main text, or it may be placed at the foot of the page.

Superior figures should be used to indicate footnotes ([1], [2], etc.). In manuscript they are marked thus:

A superior figure in the text should precede a dash, but follow every other mark of punctuation.

Where more than one footnote is likely to appear on a single page, number footnotes consecutively throughout each chapter, starting anew with superior figure 1 for the first footnote in each chapter. When a manuscript has few footnotes the numbering should start anew on each page.

In bibliographical footnotes the following forms of citation are recommended:

[1] John Gunther: *Death Be Not Proud* (New York: Harper & Brothers; 1949), pp. 110–19.

[1] Fritz Kahn: *Man in Structure and Function* (New York: Alfred A. Knopf; 1943), Vol. II, pp. 712, 732.

Or:

[1] Fritz Kahn: *Man in Structure and Function* (New York: Alfred A. Knopf; 1943), II, 712, 732.

[1] Douglass W. Orr: "A Psychoanalytic Study of a Fra-

ternal Twin," *Psychoanalytic Quarterly*, Vol. X (1941), pp. 284–96.

There is no good reason, as in a bibliography, for giving the author's surname first.

QUOTATIONS

Quotations should be carefully checked to make sure that they follow their source *literatim*, whether the style of that source corresponds in matters of usage to the style of the work in which the quotation is to appear or not. Numerous or extensive quotations from copyrighted material should be called to the publisher's attention before the manuscript is sent to the printer. Permission to use such quotations must be obtained from the copyright-owner.

PROOFS

All alterations to be made in proofs (but not in copy) must be indicated in the margin, to prevent their being missed by the printer. Take care to cross out in the text exactly — no letters or punctuation marks more or less — matter intended to be deleted or replaced by words or letters written in the margin. A caret (∧) inserted in the text indicates exactly where words or letters written in the margin are to be inserted.

INDEX

The following form of index has proved useful, though some works may, by their nature, require a special form:

Note that subheadings are listed in order of page sequence, not alphabetically; and that they are ordinarily run in.

Note that names beginning with *Mc-* follow all items beginning with *Ma-*; that abbreviations are listed as though spelled out; that complete words, like *New*, precede compound forms of it, like *Newfoundland*.

BIBLIOGRAPHY

A bibliography, when one is included, is usually arranged alphabetically by authors, the surname first. Special care should be taken to make authors' names, titles of works, and publishers' names correspond exactly to those on the title pages of works cited (including, in names of publishing companies, "& Co.," "and Company," or whatever form the company itself uses on the title page). The date of publication should always be included if possible, and the edition specified if a particular one is referred to. The following forms have proved useful:

MENCKEN, H. L.: *The American Language. An Inquiry into the Development of English in the United States.* Fourth edition. New York: Alfred A. Knopf; 1936.

——: *Treatise on Right and Wrong.* New York: Alfred A. Knopf; 1934.

STRONG, L. A. G.: "At the Barber's." *Atlantic Monthly*, Vol. CLXII, No. 2 (August 1938), pp. 208–12.

MARKS USED IN THE MARGIN
IN CORRECTING PROOFS

ဗ   Delete; omit.

c   Close up; omit space.

ဗ̃   Delete type and close up.

stet   Let it stand. (Place dots under type to be retained.)

ital   Put in italics. (Draw a line under type to be italicized.)

rom   Put in roman type. (Draw a line under type to be roman.)

¶   Make a new paragraph.

run on   Run on, without a new paragraph.

\#   Insert space.

|| Straighten lines at side of page.

⊙   Period.

=   Hyphen.

ᴧ   Apostrophe.

ᐱ   Comma.

⌐   Move to the left.

¬   Move to the right.

cap   Make capital letter. (Draw three lines under letters to
       be capitalized.)

l.c.   Make lower case. (Draw a slanting line through letters to
       be made lower case.)

sm.cap   Make small capitals. (Draw two lines under letters to be
       made small capitals.)

X   Broken letter. (Draw a line under letter in text.)

em/en   One-em or one-en dash.

PROOF SHOWING CORRECTIONS

even while he admits that the face of the country
seem covered with land grants, in the very parts men
want to settle, still coolly proposes to settle the matter
not by the courts, but by action of a Legislature which
would be under the control of the settlers *themselves*.
The very grievance that he states is so stated to show
too clearly the remedy that he had in mind. Let the
settlers, he says, 'Apply wherever they may, and to
whomsoever they may, and the result is invariably
the same: they are repulsed with an indignant, 'This
is all *mine*.' This all embracing occupant, following
the very expresive and exclusive declamation here alluded to, goes on to describe his unbounded premise.
'That mountain, says he, 'on the East is the Southeast corner of my farm, and that timbered county
which you see in the distance is my northwest corner; the other corners of my farm is rather indefinetely
marked at present, but I shall endeavour to have the
ROPE applied to them also, as soon as the ALCALDE
is at leisure.'

Well, if this indefinite state of affairs is the grievance (and it is plainly a grievance) what shall be the
thought of a man whose plan for settling the difficulty
is first of all a patent judicial examination of the traditions, usages, laws and grants under which the claims
are made, but the calling of a land hungry legislature
assembly of the intruders themselves, to apply the
precedents of the unoccupied Oregon wilderness to
the settlement of the ancient problem of california
land law. As to the facts Mr. Hastings makes the
common settlers blunder, found also in Iden's proclamation in the spring of 1846, according to which
the Mexican government has somehow guaranteed to
every American settler a tract of land immediately

even while he admits that the face of the country seems covered with land grants in the very parts where men want to settle, still coolly proposes to settle the matter, not by the courts, but by the action of a legislature that would be under the control of the settlers themselves. The very grievance that he states is so stated as to show too clearly the remedy that he has in mind: Let the settlers, he says, "apply wherever they may, and to whomsoever they may, and the result is invariably the same: they are repulsed with an indignant 'This is all mine.' This all-embracing occupant, after the very expressive and exclusive declamation here alluded to, goes on to describe his unbounded premises. 'That mountain,' says he, 'on the east is the southeast corner of my farm, and that timbered country which you see in the distance is my northwest corner; the other corners of my farm are rather indefinitely marked at present, but I shall endeavor to have the ROPE applied to them also, as soon as the ALCALDE is at leisure.' " Well, if this indefinite state of affairs is the grievance—and it is plainly a grievance—what shall be thought of a man whose plan for settling the difficulty is not first of all a patient judicial examination of the traditions, usages, laws, and grants under which these claims are made, but the calling of a land-hungry legislative assembly of the intruders themselves to apply the precedents of the unoccupied Oregon wilderness to the settlement of the ancient problems of California land law? As for the facts, Mr. Hastings makes the common settlers' blunder, found also in Ide's proclamation in the spring of 1846, according to which the Mexican government had somehow guaranteed to every American settler a tract of land immediately upon his arrival. This was a very

A SAMPLE PAGE OF MANUSCRIPT (Reduced)

Wagner used the piano now and then, as all composers do, to try out audibly what he had put on paper. But the piano sometimes served a further purpose in his case: the _sound_ of the music somehow helped him to recall, from the background of his memory, passages, and the connecting matter between passages, that he had shaped for himself in weeks or months or years gone by as he brooded over the characters and episodes of his work; it helped him, in fact, to get into the cataleptic state that is necessary for artistic creation of the finest kind. 15/

We do not lack testimony as to the "raptus" -- to employ a term that will be familiar to readers of Beethoven's life -- that descended upon Wagner also, submerged and transformed him, when he was in the thick of composition. Weissheimer has told us how, in Biebrich in 1862, he chanced to interrupt him during the composition of the _Meistersinger_.

"I knocked at his door, and as he did not answer I assumed that he had gone to the hotel to dine. I was just on the point of seeking him out there when I heard a commotion inside. I knocked again.

15/ We have his own plain testimony to this effect. He told Cosima in 1874 that "When I sit down to the piano it is only to _recall_ things: no new idea occurs to me there." See Richard Graf du Moulin Eckart: _Cosima Wagner_ (Munich, 1929, 1931), Vol. I, pp. 704/5.

INDEX OF NAMES

This index contains only the names of persons. For abstract terms and concepts and for historical processes, the reader should consult the analytical Table of Contents.

A NOTE ON THE TYPE

This book was set on the Linotype in ELECTRA, *designed by W. A. Dwiggins. The Electra face is a simple and readable type suitable for printing books by present-day processes. It is not based on any historical model, and hence does not echo any particular time or fashion. It is without eccentricities to catch the eye and interfere with reading — in general, its aim is to perform the function of a good book printing-type: to be read, and not seen.*

Typographic and binding designs are by W. A. Dwiggins.

The book was composed, printed, and bound by The Plimpton Press, Norwood, Massachusetts.